# Crafting Effective Prompts: How to Guide AI Effectively

An AI Prompt Engineering Guide with Practical Examples for Everyone

Marcel Jud, MSc.

# Legal notice/Imprint

**Title:** CRAFTING EFFECTIVE PROMPTS: An AI Prompt Engineering Guide

**Publisher:** Marcel Jud, MSc.

**Editorial deadline:** 13/11/2024

Please note that information and developments after the editorial deadline are not shown in this book.

**Self-Publisher**

**Published:** 2024

# Introduction

## Overview

In recent years, artificial intelligence has rapidly become part of our daily lives, helping us with tasks as varied as planning travel routes, generating creative content, or even offering insights into more complex topics. At the heart of this interaction with AI lies a simple yet powerful tool: the prompt. The way we frame a question, give instructions, or provide context directly impacts how effectively and accurate these generative AI models respond to us.

This book is your personal guide to mastering the art of prompting, not only with large language models (LLMs) like ChatGPT but some may also apply for other generative AI purposes like text-to-image models. By learning how to shape prompts thoughtfully, you can expect the most relevant, accurate, and creative answers. The journey begins with understanding what makes a prompt effective—things like clarity, specificity, and alignment with the task at hand. Prompt engineering is transforming how we interact with AI, especially large language models (LLMs) like ChatGPT, LLaMA, and others. These models, which can generate text, answer questions, and perform various complex tasks, depend heavily on the instructions, or "prompts," put in by users.

This book is designed to explain prompt engineering for a wide range of users—whether you're new to generative AI or looking to refine your personal prompting approach. By understanding how to construct prompts for specific tasks, guide the model's behavior, and yield precise results, readers are able to benefit from the full potential of LLMs.

Throughout the following chapters, we'll explore both foundational techniques and advanced strategies that will help you interact with LLMs in a way that feels natural and rewarding. You'll learn how to:

- Create clear, purpose-driven prompts for accurate results.
- Implement advanced strategies for complex, multi-step tasks.
- Customize prompts for specific tones, styles, and outcomes.

Whether you're a newcomer or someone looking to deepen your understanding of prompt engineering, this book is designed to make the process accessible and intuitive.

## *Purpose of the Book*

By providing a comprehensive overview of foundational techniques, best practices, examples and advanced prompting strategies, this book will help you develop a systematic approach to prompt engineering. Readers will learn how to frame tasks clearly, apply sophisticated prompting techniques to address complex situations, and ultimately enhance the quality, consistency, and relevance of AI-generated responses. Additionally, you will gain insights into how to adapt and customize prompts to different contexts, ensuring that your interactions with AI are both efficient and effective. The goal is not only to improve your interactions with AI models but also to foster creativity, problem-solving, and efficiency in a wide range of applications, from everyday tasks to more specialized professional challenges. This guide will also encourage you to experiment with different prompting methods, pushing the boundaries of what is possible with AI and unlocking new opportunities for innovation.

The book is designed for various audiences, from scientists, educators and researchers to content creators, business professionals, hobbyists and even retirees. With clear examples, practical exercises, and illustrative case studies, this guide will help you understand the nuances of prompt formulation and equip you with the tools needed to refine your prompts iteratively for optimal results. You will also find targeted advice for different use cases, whether you are looking to streamline workflows, generate creative content, or conduct in-depth research.

# ONE

## Foundations of Prompt Engineering

The journey to effective prompt engineering begins with understanding its foundations. This chapter answers the question of why prompts matter, and what are the underlying key principles of effective communication with large language models. By applying these foundational concepts, you'll be well-equipped to engage efficiently with LLMs and direct them toward the desired outcome.

### *Why Prompts Matter*

Prompts are the primary interface between users and large language models. They are instructions, questions, or context that you provide to the model in order to get a specific type of response. The quality of the responses generated is heavily influenced by how well you craft your prompts. In simple terms: *better prompts lead to better results*.

The importance of prompts can be compared with giving directions to a skilled professional. If your directions are vague or incomplete, even the most skilled professional will struggle to understand what exactly you want, and the end result may not align with your expectations. Conversely, a well-defined prompt can significantly enhance the performance of an LLM, enabling it to deliver more accurate, relevant, and unique responses.

By applying some basic principles, you can transform a general question into a precise, actionable query, ensuring the model delivers the information or solution you are looking for.

## Key Concepts: GIGO, Clarity, Specificity, and Structure

The effectiveness of a prompt is built upon several key concepts: GIGO, clarity, specificity, and structure:

**GIGO** (Garbage In, Garbage Out): This principle is borrowed from computing and is especially true for prompt engineering. If the input provided to an LLM is unclear, overly vague, or lacks context, the output will be similarly unreliable. Crafting effective prompts is about reducing ambiguity and ensuring that the input is well thought out, relevant, task-specific and precise. The better the input, the better the output. Taking the time to carefully consider the language, context, and detail in your prompt will help ensure the responses are high quality, relevant, and aligned with your expectations.

**Clarity**: Clarity is essential for effective communication with LLMs. A prompt should be straightforward, concise, and easy to understand. This helps the model "understand" your expectations without confusion or misinterpretation. Avoid overly complex language or long-winded instructions that might influence the intended meaning. Instead, break down complex tasks into simpler parts, ensuring that each part is clear and easy for the model to follow. By providing clear instructions, you minimize the risk of errors or irrelevant outputs, making your interaction with the model more efficient and productive.

**Specificity**: Specificity is another critical factor in prompt construction. The more specific you are, the better the model will understand what you need. For instance, rather than asking "Tell me about animals," you could specify, "Tell me about the habitat of African elephants."

Specificity not only helps narrow down the focus but also makes the response more useful and relevant. Being specific means providing clear boundaries and expectations, which guide the model towards delivering a targeted and informative response. This approach ensures that you get detailed, relevant information rather than a broad, generalized answer that may not fully address your needs.

Structure: Structure refers to the way you organize your prompt to guide the model's response. A well-structured prompt might include delimiters, numbered steps, or explicit instructions that make it easy for the model to follow your intent. For example, specifying "Step 1, Step 2, Step 3" can lead to a more organized and logical response, particularly for complex tasks or multi-part questions. Even a simple instruction, like "do it step-by-step" enables the model to give a more structured, streamlined output. Structuring your prompt effectively helps the model understand the sequence and hierarchy of the information you are seeking, which can lead to more coherent and comprehensive answers. Proper structure is especially important for multi-step tasks or when you need the model to address several aspects of a topic in a specific order.

Understanding and applying these foundational concepts will significantly improve your experience with LLMs. As you progress through this book, you will encounter practical examples that will help you put these concepts into practice to strengthen your ability to craft effective prompts that yield expected results.

**Crafting Your First Prompts**

Let's start by crafting a few basic prompts. These exercises will help you practice the principles of clarity, specificity, and structure. Consider the following examples:

**Example 1:** Unclear Prompt

"Tell me something about climate change."

Improved Prompt

"Explain the primary causes of climate change, focusing on human activities and their impact on global temperatures."

**Example 2:** Vague Prompt

"How does technology affect society?"

**Improved Prompt**

"Describe three ways that mobile technology has influenced social interactions in the past decade, both positively and negatively. Explain your reasoning"

**Example 3:** Lacking Structure

"Give me advice on improving my fitness."

**Improved Prompt**

"Provide a three-part plan to improve overall fitness, including aerobic exercises, strength training, and dietary recommendations."

Through these examples, notice how adding specific details and clear instructions transforms a vague question into a targeted, actionable prompt that will guide the LLM to produce a more meaningful and informative response.

**The Role of Experimentation**

Prompt engineering is not an exact science, and there is often no one-size-fits-all solution. Experimentation is a core part of the process. You may need to iterate on a prompt multiple times before you achieve the desired response. This trial-and-error approach is natural and expected, and it often leads to discovering new and innovative ways to communicate in a clear and effective way with LLMs.

To be effective at prompt engineering, you should feel comfortable experimenting, adjusting phrasing, testing different levels of detail, and combining various prompting techniques. Throughout this book, we will explore a variety of approaches that you can use to refine your prompts and improve your outcomes. The more you experiment, the better you'll understand how the model interprets different inputs, allowing you to fine-tune your prompts for optimal performance.

**Summary**

The foundations of prompt engineering lies in understanding why prompts matter and how key concepts like GIGO, clarity, specificity, and structure influence the quality of responses from LLMs. By focusing on these foundational elements, you will be better equipped to communicate effectively with AI models, improving both the relevance and quality of their responses. As we move forward, we'll build upon these principles, diving deeper into essential prompting strategies and techniques that will help you.

# System vs. User Prompts – Understanding Their Roles

When working with large language models (LLMs), it is crucial to understand the distinction between system prompts and user prompts. Think of these as two distinct voices guiding the model: the system prompt is the architect, laying down the foundational blueprint for the model's behavior, while the user prompt provides specific instructions for individual tasks. Both types are essential for effective communication with LLMs and play a key role in obtaining the best possible results. Understanding how each type of prompt works, and how they work together, can significantly enhance the quality, consistency, and appropriateness of the outputs you receive.

A helpful way to conceptualize these prompt types is to imagine a play being performed. In this analogy, the system prompt is the director, setting the stage, defining the character traits, and establishing the tone for the performance. The user prompt, on the other hand, serves as the script—detailing the specific lines and actions for each scene. The interplay between these two elements shapes how the model behaves and what responses are generated. The better you understand and control these prompts, the more powerful and refined your interactions with the LLM become.

Consider the system prompt as the backstage crew, making sure everything is set before the curtain rises. It arranges the foundation, ensuring that the lighting, props, and cues are properly configured. The user prompt, by contrast, is the actor stepping into the spotlight— interpreting the director's vision and adding a personal touch to deliver an engaging performance. This analogy underscores the importance of both prompts working in harmony; when they align well, the resulting "performance" can be both seamless and impressive.

In this chapter, we will dive deeper into both system and user prompts, exploring their influence on the model's behavior and how they can be strategically combined for optimal outcomes. We will provide practical examples, highlight common pitfalls, and share useful tips to help you make the most of each prompt type. By the end of this chapter, you will have a comprehensive understanding of how to effectively use system and user prompts to create dynamic and well-targeted interactions with the model.

## *System Prompts: Structuring the Model's Role and Tone*

System prompts serve as the backbone of any interaction with large language models. They establish the context, shape the model's behavior, and effectively determine how the model generates responses. If you've ever wondered why a model's reply sounds authoritative, empathetic, or technical, it's often because of the system prompt that set the initial direction. A well-crafted system prompt helps define the model's role, the tone of the conversation, and the guiding principles it should adhere to throughout the interaction.

Imagine you are using an LLM for a customer service task. In this scenario, a system prompt might define the model as an empathetic support agent. You could start by instructing it with: "You are a friendly and knowledgeable customer service representative who helps customers resolve issues quickly and effectively." This prompt creates a solid foundation for the model's responses, ensuring they are polite, informative, and solution-oriented. Without this underlying prompt, the model's behavior could become inconsistent, potentially shifting from overly formal to oddly casual, which would negatively impact the user experience.

The beauty of system prompts lies in their ability to instill consistency. By setting a system-level directive, you create a reliable framework that persists across multiple interactions. For example, if you are using the LLM to assist with scientific research, you could specify: "You are a research assistant well-versed in the latest advancements in artificial intelligence and neuroscience. Provide evidence-based responses and maintain a professional tone." With such a prompt, you ensure that every response meets a scientific standard, reducing the risk of casual or irrelevant remarks that might distract or confuse the user.

Another example of a system prompt involves structuring a model's tone for educational purposes. Suppose you're designing an app to help children learn about space. The system prompt might read: "You are a friendly and engaging space explorer who loves to teach young children all about the wonders of the universe in a simple and fun way." This kind of system prompt doesn't just establish factual accuracy; it ensures that the model communicates in a way that's exciting, accessible, and age-appropriate for young learners. It allows the model to maintain a consistent voice that aligns with the educational goals of the interaction.

System prompts are particularly powerful when applied to complex or sensitive scenarios. For instance, if an LLM is being used in a mental health context, the system prompt could be something like: "You are a compassionate and non-judgmental listener, providing thoughtful responses that prioritize the well-being of the individual." This helps the model maintain an appropriate tone, avoid giving medical advice, and ensure that its responses remain empathetic and supportive—crucial elements when dealing with emotionally sensitive topics.

The key strength of system prompts is their ability to guide the model toward a specific behavioral pattern, maintaining this direction consistently across different user interactions. This kind of guidance ensures that the model doesn't steer into territory that may be irrelevant or inappropriate. For example, in a customer service context, where friendliness and helpfulness are crucial, a consistent system prompt ensures that even when the user asks an unexpected or challenging question, the model responds within the established tone and role.

By carefully crafting system prompts, you set the underlying tone and guidelines that align the model's behavior with your specific needs. This makes the model not just a tool, but an active participant that understands the kind of role it is supposed to play. Whether it's offering customer support, engaging young learners, assisting with research, or providing empathetic listening, a strong system prompt creates a scaffold upon which all user prompts can effectively build.

In the next section, we'll explore how user prompts add an extra layer of specificity, allowing you to craft precise, goal-oriented interactions on top of this structured foundation.

## User Prompts: Crafting Effective Inputs for Desired Outcomes

While system prompts define the structural framework for an AI's response, user prompts play a vital role in crafting specific and nuanced interactions. Essentially, user prompts are the detailed instructions you provide to steer the AI toward your intended goals. Think of them as the guiding questions or commands that you, as the user, employ to shape the behavior and content of the model's output. In this section, we'll learn how to craft effective user prompts and explore practical strategies for getting the most accurate and meaningful responses.

### Understanding User Prompts

User prompts are what directly inform the model about the task at hand. For example, if a system prompt sets the AI's persona as an expert chef, a user prompt might ask, "What are some creative uses for leftover risotto?" This prompt guides the model to generate a specific type of response, leveraging its 'chef' persona to provide relevant and contextually appropriate ideas.

The effectiveness of user prompts depends on clarity, specificity, and structure. Vague prompts often result in equally vague responses, whereas more specific prompts encourage detailed and informative outputs. For example, instead of asking, "Tell me about health," a more refined prompt like "Explain the health benefits of regular aerobic exercise for adults" will generate a far more focused and useful answer.

**The Role of Specificity and Context**

An effective user prompt includes not only the main request but also the surrounding context that helps the model understand your expectations. Imagine you're working on a historical essay and need information about the Renaissance. You could phrase your user prompt in a basic way, like, "Tell me about the Renaissance." This will certainly yield information, but it may be too general. Instead, try a more nuanced prompt such as, "Describe the impact of the Renaissance on scientific thinking in Europe, particularly focusing on Galileo and Copernicus." By adding these contextual cues, you provide a focus for the model, ensuring that the response meets your specific needs.

A practical example might be when you're writing a marketing blog post about eco-friendly products. A prompt like, "Write a paragraph about eco-friendly products," may produce a generic result. But if you modify it to, "Write a paragraph that explains how eco-friendly cleaning products benefit both the environment and human health, focusing on ingredients like vinegar and baking soda," you'll end up with a response that's both richer in detail and more on-point.

## Techniques for Crafting Effective User Prompts

There are several techniques that can elevate the quality of your user prompts, each suited to different types of outcomes:

1. Directive Language: Use clear, actionable language to make sure your intent is understood. Instead of phrasing prompts passively, like "Can you provide...," try directives like "Provide," "List," or "Explain." For instance, "List three effective ways to reduce screen time for children under 12." This ensures the AI understands exactly what action to take and avoids ambiguity.

2. Audience Specification: If the response needs to target a particular audience, include that in your prompt. A prompt like "Explain blockchain" will produce a different output than "Explain blockchain to someone without a tech background." Defining the audience helps the AI adjust the language and complexity of the answer accordingly. This is particularly useful when dealing with technical subjects or complex concepts that need to be tailored to different levels of expertise.

3. Encouraging Depth: When the goal is a detailed response, directly ask for it. Instead of a prompt like, "What causes climate change?" opt for "Provide a detailed explanation of both natural and human-induced causes of climate change, including examples." By signaling the depth you want, the AI can prioritize elaboration. This approach works well for educational content or in-depth articles where comprehensive coverage is required.

4. Step-by-Step Requests: To ensure thorough coverage of complex topics, ask the model to think step by step. For instance, "Explain the process of photosynthesis step by step, starting from sunlight absorption to the production of glucose." This makes the response more organized and easier to follow, which is especially beneficial for explaining procedures or multi-step processes.

5. Using Delimiters: For situations where you need a specific format, delimiters are your best friend. A prompt that reads, "### Task: Write a concise summary of renewable energy technologies ### Details: Focus on solar, wind, and geothermal energy, and mention their respective advantages" provides clear sections that guide the response structure. This is particularly helpful when you need consistency in output format, such as in data collection or formal documentation.

## Real-Life Application of User Prompts

Imagine you're working in customer service for an e-commerce business, and you need the AI to draft an email response to a customer inquiry. A basic prompt like "Write a customer service response" might not yield the most suitable result. Instead, you could craft the prompt as follows: "Write a polite email response to a customer named John who wants to return a product that was damaged during delivery. Apologize for the inconvenience and provide instructions on how he can proceed with the return."

This revised prompt provides the model with specific details about the scenario, enabling it to craft a response that is empathetic, informative, and relevant to the situation. The more context and direction you give, the more the AI can tailor the response to meet the customer's needs effectively.

Another practical example could involve content creation for social media. Say you're managing a brand's Instagram account and need a caption for a post about an upcoming sale. A generic prompt like "Write a caption for a sale" may result in something unsuitable. However, if you specify, "Write an engaging Instagram caption for a weekend sale offering 20% off on all home decor items, and include a call to action encouraging followers to click the link in bio," the resulting caption will be more targeted and compelling.

User prompts are the bridge between your goals and the AI's capabilities. Crafting these prompts thoughtfully makes a huge difference in the quality of interaction you experience. Whether you're working on creative writing, technical documentation, or customer service, refining user prompts to be specific, directive, and context-rich helps in achieving more precise and impactful results.

## Combining System and User Prompts for Enhanced Interactions

Now that we have a thorough understanding of both system and user prompts, let's explore how to effectively combine them. When used together, system and user prompts become an incredibly powerful duo, allowing you to shape both the model's personality and the specifics of its output. Think of them as the dynamic duo of prompting: the system prompt provides the overall direction and mindset of the AI, while the user prompt focuses on specific tasks and details. This combination lets you achieve the perfect balance between broad, consistent behavior and tailored, detailed responses.

Imagine interacting with an AI to develop marketing content for a new product. A system prompt might set the AI's tone and perspective by stating, "You are an experienced marketing expert with a creative personality." This prompt lays the foundation for the AI's responses, defining the approach it should take for all subsequent tasks. After establishing this foundational mindset, you can then issue user prompts like, "Write a social media post promoting a new eco-friendly water bottle. Focus on sustainability and include a playful call to action." Here, the user prompt draws on the persona already established by the system prompt, resulting in an output that is not only relevant to the task but also carries a consistent voice and tone that matches your marketing goals.

In scenarios where consistency across a series of responses is crucial—such as customer service, educational content, or brand messaging. The synergy between system and user prompts ensures that each response follows the established tone while effectively addressing specific needs. This method is particularly valuable for maintaining uniformity across multiple outputs without sacrificing the personalization that makes responses more engaging and meaningful.

Let's take another example: Suppose you're building an AI tutor to help students learn algebra. The system prompt could be, "You are a patient and friendly algebra tutor who explains concepts in a simple and relatable way." The user prompt could then be, "Explain how to solve a quadratic equation step by step, assuming the student is just starting to learn algebra." By combining these prompts, you ensure that the explanation is both approachable and aligned with the intended teaching style. This pairing of system and user prompts effectively shapes the AI into an ideal tutor for a beginner—someone who is supportive, clear, and educational, making the learning process less intimidating and more accessible for the student.

Combining system and user prompts is also effective in professional contexts where a consistent tone is required, such as drafting legal documents, writing formal letters, or generating official reports. For instance, setting a system prompt like, "You are a formal and precise legal assistant," lays the groundwork for any specific user prompt that follows. Suppose a user prompt then asks, "Draft a letter requesting a client to submit missing documents for their case." The output will not only reflect the request but will also maintain a formal and professional tone suitable for a legal context, helping to achieve the desired level of professionalism and ensuring clarity.

Another practical scenario could be content creation for a health and wellness blog. You might use a system prompt like, "You are a knowledgeable wellness coach who provides friendly, actionable advice on healthy living." Once this tone is set, you could follow up with a user prompt like, "Write an engaging article about the benefits of yoga for stress relief, including practical tips for beginners." The resulting output will be infused with the warmth and expertise of a wellness coach, while the content will be directly tailored to the specific topic at hand. This approach ensures that the content is not only accurate but also approachable and engaging for readers who are looking to improve their well-being.

In customer service settings, combining system and user prompts can be particularly impactful. A system prompt might be, "You are a helpful and empathetic customer service representative who prioritizes solving customer issues in a friendly manner." This sets the overarching tone, while user prompts can address specific scenarios, such as, "Provide a response to a customer who is upset about a delayed shipment, and offer them a discount on their next order." By combining these prompts, the AI can craft a response that is both empathetic and solution-oriented, ensuring that the customer feels heard and valued.

In summary, system prompts and user prompts are the yin and yang of effective AI communication. System prompts guide the general attitude, persona, and style of the model, while user prompts give specific, actionable instructions for particular tasks. Using these tools in combination allows you to not only control the overall persona of the model but also ensure that individual responses are perfectly tuned to meet the specific needs of the moment. It's like driving a car—the system prompt is the steering wheel that sets the direction, while the user prompt is the accelerator that moves you forward in a controlled, intentional way. With both working together, you'll find yourself navigating smoothly to your destination, achieving results that are both consistent and precisely tailored to your goals.

*Advanced AI platforms often have separate fields for system prompts and user prompts. For example, a system prompt may set the AI to "act as a math tutor," while user prompts ask specific questions. These features are common in tools like GPT Playground or chatbot configurations, enabling further customization.*

**NOTE**

# TWO

## Core Strategies for Effective Prompting

Now that we've laid the groundwork in Chapter 1, let's dive further into prompt engineering strategies. Imagine you're learning how to cook yourself a delicious meal: you've got the ingredients, but now you need to learn the techniques to make a Michelin-star dish. This chapter is all about refining those techniques—learning how to properly season, simmer, and sauté your prompts to perfection. We'll explore ways to be direct, define your audience, add flavorful examples, break down complex tasks like a recipe, and more, to ensure that you serve up a prompt that the LLM can truly sink its teeth into. And don't worry if you burn a few attempts—prompt engineering is like cooking, it's all about experimenting until you get it just right (minus the messy kitchen).

### *Directness: Get Straight to the Point*

When it comes to interacting with LLMs, it's important to be direct. Extra words may be appreciated in human conversations, but with LLMs, it's best to avoid unnecessary pleasantries. The more concise and clear your request, the better the result. That doesn't mean, that it is bad to say please or thanks, of course ;-)

Think of it like placing an order at a busy coffee shop—you want to be clear and quick to ensure you get exactly what you want without any confusion. Instead of saying, "Could you please provide a summary of climate change, if you don't mind?" simply say, "Provide a summary of climate change." Directness helps the LLM understand your intentions immediately, leading to more efficient and accurate responses.

## Define Your Audience

One of the simplest yet most powerful strategies to enhance the effectiveness of your prompt is specifying the audience. Imagine trying to tell a joke to a toddler versus a stand-up comedy crowd—same content, but vastly different deliveries. The same concept applies when interacting with LLMs. If you don't specify the audience, the model may just make assumptions, and assumptions often lead to "meh" results. Are you addressing a group of experts in quantum mechanics, or are you trying to explain the concept to a high school student? The difference is key.

**Example:**

- General Prompt: "Explain quantum entanglement."
- Defined Audience Prompt: "Explain quantum entanglement to a high school student with no prior physics knowledge."
- Expert-Level Prompt: "Provide a detailed explanation of quantum entanglement suitable for a graduate-level physics course."

By defining the audience, you help the LLM understand the context and adjust its tone, complexity, and the amount of detail provided. This makes it more likely that the response will be audience appropriate.

**Use Example-Driven Prompting**

Examples are like guiding lights that help steer LLMs toward the response you want. Including relevant examples in your prompt can act like a GPS for the model, helping it understand where you want to go.

**Example:**

- Basic Prompt: "Write a story about a hero."
- Example-Driven Prompt: "Write a story about a hero. For example, the hero should be someone ordinary who discovers their power by helping others."

By providing an example, you give the model a frame of reference, helping it narrow down the scope of potential responses and align more closely with your vision. It's like saying, "Hey, not just any hero—this kind of hero."

**Break Down Complex Tasks**

Complex tasks can be overwhelming, not just for people, but also for language models. When faced with a huge mountain of information to climb, it's often best to break it into smaller hills, taking them step-by-step. This makes it easier for the LLM to process and gives you a better, more comprehensive output.

**Example:**

- General Prompt: "Explain the process of photosynthesis and its role in the ecosystem."
- Broken-Down Prompt: "First, explain the steps involved in photosynthesis, including the role of chlorophyll. Next,

describe how photosynthesis impacts the ecosystem, focusing on oxygen production and its importance to other organisms."

Breaking down the task allows the LLM to provide more focused and thorough responses, reducing the likelihood of missing key details or producing incomplete information. It's like asking for directions one turn at a time instead of trying to remember the entire route.

**Specify the Format and Scope**

Imagine ordering a meal at a restaurant without mentioning whether you want it to-go or served on a fancy platter. You might get exactly what you ordered, but it might not be presented the way you intended. The same goes for LLMs—specifying the desired format or scope can make a huge difference.

**Example:**

- Vague Prompt: "Tell me about the benefits of exercise."
- Specified Format and Scope: "List the top five benefits of aerobic exercise in bullet points, including physical and mental health benefits."

When you specify the format, the LLM can structure the output accordingly, making it easier to read and more practical for your intended use. It's like choosing between a well-organized shopping list and a random collection of items scrawled on a napkin.

**Encourage Step-by-Step Reasoning**

For prompts involving logical or complex reasoning, encouraging the model to think step-by-step could be a game-changer. This approach is particularly helpful for problem-solving or decision-making scenarios (even though there is no classic "reasoning" in LLMs but that's another story).

**Example:**

- General Prompt: "How can we solve the issue of climate change?"
- Step-by-Step Prompt: "Explain, step-by-step, how we can mitigate climate change. Start by discussing the role of renewable energy sources, then move on to reducing carbon emissions in transportation, and conclude with individual behavioral changes that can make a difference."

Step-by-step prompts guide the model through a logical sequence of points, resulting in a more coherent and comprehensive response. It's like assembling IKEA furniture—one step at a time leads to a well-put-together product (hopefully).

## Clarify Ambiguities

Ambiguity can lead to suboptimal responses. If there's any aspect of your prompt that could be interpreted in multiple ways, clarify it. It's like asking someone to bring "the thing" from the other room—you'll probably end up with something you didn't want.

**Example:**

- Ambiguous Prompt: "Tell me about Python."
- Clarified Prompt: "Tell me about Python, the programming language, including its main features and popular applications."

Without such clarification, the model might misunderstand whether you're referring to the programming language or the snake, leading to irrelevant or mixed information. Clarity helps avoid that awkward moment when you get a 10-page essay on reptiles instead of coding.

## *Experiment and Iterate*

Prompt engineering is a lot like trying on clothes—you have to keep changing until you find the perfect fit. Sometimes the initial prompt doesn't yield what you need, and that's perfectly okay. Iteratively refining your prompts is key to get the desired output.

**Example:**

- Initial Prompt: "Describe renewable energy."
- Refined Prompt: "Describe renewable energy sources, such as solar, wind, and hydroelectric power, including their benefits and challenges compared to fossil fuels."

Each iteration helps you understand how the model processes different inputs, allowing you to gradually home in on the optimal prompt that yields the best response. Think of it as whittling down a rough piece of wood into a polished sculpture—each pass makes it better.

## Summary

Effective prompting requires more than just asking questions; it requires a thoughtful approach that includes being direct, defining the audience, providing examples, breaking down complex tasks, specifying format and scope, encouraging step-by-step thinking, and clarifying ambiguities. By employing these core strategies, you can maximize the utility of large language models, obtaining responses that are not only accurate but also well-suited to your very own, specific needs.

In the next chapter, we will explore advanced prompting techniques that further enhance the quality of interactions with LLMs, including methods like formatting, few-shot learning, context chaining, and reinforcement of desired outputs. So, get ready to level up your prompt engineering skills—because we're just getting started!

# THREE

## Prompt Formatting Techniques

Creating effective prompts involves more than simply knowing what to ask for—it's also about how you ask it. In this chapter, we'll take a detailed look at various formatting techniques that make your prompts clearer, more structured, and ultimately more effective. We'll cover using delimiters, optimizing formatting for clarity, and the strategic repetition of key terms. These formatting tools not only help the model understand your intent but also ensure the output meets your expectations consistently. Whether you're crafting a complex query or simply want to enhance the accuracy of your answers, understanding these formatting techniques are key to generate expected outputs. Let's explore each technique in-depth, beginning with delimiters.

### *Using Delimiters*

Delimiters are another powerful tool in prompt engineering, and they act as clear markers to separate different components of a prompt. This becomes particularly valuable when you're working on complex prompts that contain multiple instructions, examples, or need to provide structured information to the model. Delimiters, such as double slashes (//), hashtags (###), or brackets, serve to enhance readability and guide the model effectively.

Imagine you want the model to generate a summary and answer questions based on a provided passage. Instead of throwing everything together, you can use delimiters to distinctly mark each part:

### Text to summarize ###

Artificial Intelligence (AI) has revolutionized many sectors, including healthcare, education, and entertainment. By enabling predictive algorithms, personalized content, and automation, AI has reshaped our interaction with technology and each other.

### Task ###

1. Summarize the above text in one sentence.

2. Provide two examples of AI applications in healthcare.

Here, the use of "###" makes it easy for the model to identify each section. It improves the organization of your prompt, resulting in more accurate and reliable outputs. It's like telling the model: "Here is what I need you to focus on right now." Without delimiters, the prompt can appear overwhelming and chaotic, making it harder for the model to discern which instruction pertains to which part of the content.

Another great use of delimiters is when you need to include additional information that you don't want the model to confuse with your main question. For instance, in technical or code-related prompts:

### Instruction ###

Create a Python function that takes a list of integers and returns the sum.

### Example Input ###

[1, 2, 3, 4]

### Expected Output ###

10

In this example, each element of the prompt is clearly divided, helping the model focus on one specific aspect of the task at a time. Such separation ensures that the model treats your question with the precision you intend. Delimiters, therefore, act as guideposts—much like an instructional manual with clear chapters and sections.

Another scenario where delimiters come in handy is when dealing with long or multi-part instructions. Imagine you are creating an instructional prompt for a multi-step process, such as setting up a database:

### Step 1: Install Database Software ###

Provide the steps to install PostgreSQL on a Windows machine.

### Step 2: Configure the Database ###

Explain how to configure the PostgreSQL server for optimal performance.

### Step 3: Create User Accounts ###

List the commands needed to create a new database user with read and write permissions.

By breaking down the task into distinct sections, you make it far easier for the model to process each instruction and provide accurate, detailed responses. Without such segmentation, the model might struggle to differentiate between each step, leading to incomplete or confusing outputs.

Delimiters can also help when dealing with prompts that involve providing a large amount of context before posing a question. By maintaining order, delimiters ensure that the flow of logic remains intact. This also means that when you revise or refine your prompt, you can quickly isolate the sections that need tweaking without losing the overall coherence of the message.

In addition, delimiters prove invaluable when providing examples alongside instructions.

**For example:**

### Instruction ###

Write a function that calculates the factorial of a number.

### Example ###

Input: 5

Output: 120

Here, separating the instruction from the example helps the model treat the example as a reference rather than part of the task itself. It reduces ambiguity and ensures that the model knows exactly which part to execute.

Delimiters not only help the model understand the structure of your prompt, but they also make it easier for you to iterate on and improve your prompts. When you can clearly see where one section ends and another begins, editing becomes a much simpler process. This can save time, especially when you're testing multiple variations to see which prompt yields the best results.

In the next section, we will discuss another essential formatting technique—how to optimize the format for clarity, ensuring that each prompt is easy for the model to interpret accurately.


## *Formatting for Clarity*

When communicating with an LLM, clarity is king. Unlike human beings, who can draw from shared experiences or read subtle cues, an LLM relies purely on the instructions and context you provide. Formatting plays a pivotal role in ensuring that your prompts are not just readable, but also interpretable in the precise way you intend. Let's explore the different techniques to format prompts for maximal clarity.

**Why Formatting Matters**

Think of prompt formatting as akin to good punctuation in written language. Proper formatting helps understanding the purpose, structure, and relationships of different parts of the prompt clearly, allowing the model to respond in an optimal manner. By creating well-formatted prompts, you minimize the chances of misinterpretation, which can lead to irrelevant, incomplete, or even confusing outputs.

Imagine asking someone to do multiple tasks in a disorganized manner: "Can you write a summary and explain the concept and make it short and, oh, also provide some examples?" It's easy to see how this could confuse someone. LLMs face the same challenge when prompts aren't clearly structured. Proper formatting provides the equivalent of pauses, breaks, and emphasis, guiding the LLM to the response you desire.

**Structured Sections for Better Understanding**

Breaking a prompt into clear sections helps the model understand the task flow. Use headings, numbered lists, or bullet points to outline tasks in a structured manner. Just as with a well-written report, the more you break things down logically, the easier it will be for the LLM to follow the sequence.

Instead of writing:

"Explain climate change causes, give recent data, and then conclude with potential actions we can take."

Try structuring it like this:

- Task 1: Explain the causes of climate change in simple terms.
- Task 2: Provide recent statistical data (2020-2024) that supports these causes.
- Task 3: Conclude by suggesting potential actions individuals and governments can take.

This not only makes the request clearer for the LLM, but it also helps you keep track of the response structure you're expecting.

**Visual Cues for Emphasis**

Use formatting techniques such as bolding, underlining, or ALL CAPS to emphasize specific aspects of your prompt. When you emphasize certain words or phrases, it tells the LLM what elements to prioritize.

**Example:**

- "List the three MAIN benefits of adopting renewable energy sources."
- "Explain the difference between machine learning and deep learning in simple terms."

These visual cues work as highlighters, helping the LLM focus on specific components, just as a reader would zero in on bolded or highlighted text.

## Line Breaks to Indicate Different Segments

Using line breaks between different instructions or segments in your prompt can greatly enhance clarity, especially when you have a complex or multi-step request. This technique separates different parts of the instruction, so they don't get jumbled together, which is helpful for both you and the model.

**Example:**

Instead of:

"Translate the following sentence to Spanish and then summarize the translation."

Use:

- Translate the following sentence to Spanish: "The swift fox jumps over the lazy dog."
- Summarize the translated sentence in one line.

This makes it explicitly clear to the model that there are two distinct tasks that need to be executed in sequence.

## Emphasizing Context with Tags

Tags are another useful formatting technique. Tags act like labels that identify the purpose or type of content you're dealing with. This method is particularly effective when prompting LLMs to generate various types of outputs in one go.

**Example:**

### Instruction ###

Provide a brief history of artificial intelligence.

### Summary ###

Summarize the key developments mentioned in 3-4 sentences.

### Opinion ###

What are the potential future impacts of artificial intelligence on society?

This way of formatting segments into clearly tagged components helps ensure that each piece of the response is tailored to the intended request. It provides a clear outline for both the model and yourself.

**Keeping it Simple**

A good rule of thumb in formatting is: keep it simple. Too many formatting elements can be as confusing as none. Don't overload the prompt with excessive bolding, bullet points, or tags. Use formatting selectively to enhance clarity, but always keep readability in mind.

**Example of Formatting Gone Wrong**

"### TASK ### WRITE AN ESSAY ### SUMMARY ### GIVE A SUMMARY ### INSIGHT ### YOUR THOUGHTS"

The overuse of tags here doesn't aid in clarity—in fact, it confuses the LLM. The model might struggle to discern the exact order of tasks or the relationship between them.

**Instead, try simplifying:**

### Task ###

Write an essay on the benefits of renewable energy.

### Summary ###

Summarize the key points of the essay in 3-4 sentences.

### Insight ###

Provide your thoughts on the importance of adopting renewable energy.

The cleaner, more organized version leaves little room for misinterpretation.

**Practical Takeaway**

When formatting prompts, think of how you would communicate if you wanted to ensure that every detail is understood perfectly. Use headings, line breaks, bullet points, tags, and emphasis wisely to help the LLM "see" the same divisions, importance, and structure that you see. In doing so, you'll find that the model is far more likely to give you organized, relevant, and comprehensive responses.

Formatting is the foundation of prompt clarity—it's like the frame of a picture that helps display the content at its best. By carefully considering how you structure your prompts, you maximize the chances of getting an effective, high-quality output.

## Repetition of Key Terms

Repetition is an often-underestimated but powerful technique that can help guide an LLM toward more precise and focused outputs. Just as repetition helps human readers to better grasp central themes and significant points of a text, it serves to keep LLMs on track, focusing on the key concepts that should remain prominent throughout the response. By repeating key terms, you reinforce the importance of these ideas, ensuring they are clearly understood and remain the focal point of the response.

### Reinforcing the Message

When you repeat key terms, it reinforces their importance to the model, signaling that these are the concepts it should focus on. This technique is especially useful when you need the response to revolve around a central idea or when different parts of the prompt are related to the same topic. Repeating key words is akin to putting up signposts along a path, ensuring that the model follows the desired direction without deviating. This is especially critical for maintaining accuracy when the prompt is lengthy or covers multiple subtopics.

For instance, if your prompt is about sustainability, repeating the term "sustainability" throughout different sections of the prompt can help ensure that the response remains anchored to that key concept. Without this repetition, the LLM might deviate, especially if the prompt is complex or covers multiple facets. Repetition acts as a guidepost, keeping the model aligned with the main topic and preventing it from veering off into unrelated areas. This simple but effective strategy is invaluable in guiding the LLM to produce responses that are not only on-topic but also insightful and cohesive.

**Example:**

"Describe the importance of sustainability in modern agriculture. Focus on how sustainability helps reduce waste, improves soil health, and contributes to long-term productivity. Sustainability should be the central theme in your explanation."

The repetition of "sustainability" makes it clear to the LLM that this is the core topic, and every part of the response should tie back to it. By emphasizing the key term multiple times, you minimize the risk of the model focusing on secondary or unrelated topics, thereby ensuring a more cohesive and directed response. Repeating these key terms strategically helps to form a clear mental map for the LLM, reducing ambiguity and increasing the overall quality of the output.

**Creating a Narrative Thread**

Repetition also helps in creating a cohesive narrative thread throughout the response. When the same term or phrase appears multiple times, it acts as a link that ties different parts of the answer together. This is especially helpful when dealing with longer prompts or when multiple points need to be addressed that are all connected by a central theme. By repeating key terms, the response becomes more integrated and easier to follow, allowing for a more in-depth exploration of the topic.

Consider how repetition works in storytelling or persuasive writing: key ideas are often repeated to keep them fresh in the reader's mind and to reinforce their importance. The same principle applies when working with LLMs. By repeating important terms, you ensure that these elements remain prominent and are woven throughout the model's output, resulting in a unified and consistent response. A well-constructed prompt that uses repetition effectively can make the difference between a response that feels disjointed and one that is compelling and easy to understand.

**Example:**

"Explain the process of photosynthesis, highlighting the role of sunlight. Emphasize how sunlight is absorbed by chlorophyll and how sunlight drives the production of glucose. Throughout your explanation, make it clear that sunlight is the primary energy source."

By repeating "sunlight," the prompt ensures that the model will consistently highlight its role throughout the response, creating a cohesive and focused explanation. This technique helps maintain a consistent emphasis, thereby improving the quality and relevance of the response. Repetition is like a thread that binds different ideas together, forming a cohesive whole and reinforcing the core message. It keeps the response organized and ensures that the emphasis remains where it is needed most.

## Balancing Repetition with Clarity

While repetition is useful, it's important not to overdo it. Excessive repetition can make the prompt cumbersome and even confusing, leading to responses that feel redundant or overly simplistic. The key is to repeat strategically—enough to emphasize the importance of a term, but not so much that it overwhelms the prompt or the reader. Strategic repetition strikes a balance between clarity and emphasis, ensuring that the key ideas are repeated enough to be impactful without being overwhelming.

## Example of Overuse:

"Explain the importance of sustainability. Sustainability is crucial for the environment. Sustainability also helps in reducing carbon emissions. Sustainability improves resource efficiency."

In this example, the repetition is too frequent and doesn't add value. Instead, try:

"Explain the importance of sustainability for the environment, particularly how it helps reduce carbon emissions and improve resource efficiency."

Here, the term "sustainability" is still central, but its repetition is more natural and doesn't detract from the readability of the prompt. It's important to strike the right balance—using repetition to reinforce key points without making the language cumbersome or awkward. When repetition feels forced, it can distract the model and lead to outputs that lack depth or sound mechanical. Finding the right balance requires practice, but when done well, it greatly enhances the prompt's effectiveness.

**Using Synonyms to Avoid Redundancy**

One effective way to maintain focus without excessive repetition is to use synonyms or related terms. This helps reinforce the concept while keeping the language varied and interesting. By mixing in synonyms, you can maintain the emphasis on key ideas without making the prompt feel monotonous or overly repetitive. Synonyms provide a fresh way to reintroduce a concept, ensuring that it remains at the forefront of the response without becoming tiresome or repetitive.

**Example:**

"Discuss the importance of sustainability. Highlight how environmental conservation and resource efficiency—both key aspects of sustainable practices—play a role in combating climate change."

By using terms like "environmental conservation" and "resource efficiency," you keep the core idea of sustainability at the forefront while avoiding monotonous repetition. This approach keeps the language fresh and engaging while still emphasizing the main concept. It's a way to keep the LLM focused on the theme while ensuring that the response remains dynamic and nuanced. This balance between repetition and variety helps create responses that are informative, engaging, and aligned with your objectives.

## Practical Takeaway

Repetition is a valuable tool in prompt formatting that, when used strategically, can significantly enhance the clarity and cohesiveness of an LLM's response. It helps the model identify central themes and ensures that these themes are consistently addressed throughout the response. However, balance is key—repeat enough to emphasize, but not so much that it becomes redundant or distracting. Using repetition in a mindful way ensures that the output is both clear and detailed, guiding the LLM to produce content that is tightly aligned with your expectations.

Use repetition thoughtfully to keep key concepts front and center, guiding the model to produce responses that are well-aligned with your intended focus. When combined with other formatting techniques, repetition can greatly enhance the effectiveness of your prompts, leading to outputs that are both precise and comprehensive. Remember, repetition is not just about emphasis—it's about creating a coherent and connected response that keeps the reader (or model) focused on what truly matters. When used well, it is one of the most effective tools for ensuring clarity, consistency, and depth in LLM outputs.

To make the output more cohesive and to ensure that key ideas are reinforced appropriately, consider incorporating repetition alongside other prompt structuring strategies. By doing so, you set up the LLM for success, providing it with the guidance needed to deliver a response that is thorough, insightful, and fully aligned with your objectives.

# FOUR

## Practical Prompting Techniques for Specific Outcomes

As you by now already know, working with large language models, the end result is only as good as the prompt that you provide. Different outcomes require different techniques, and understanding how to structure prompts for specific goals can be the key to unlocking the full potential of these AI systems. In this chapter, we'll explore practical prompting techniques that can help you get precisely the kind of response you need from a language model. We'll cover three essential methods: step-by-step prompts, example-driven prompts, and using output primers. Each of these techniques is geared towards achieving clarity, precision, and effective outcomes. Whether you're trying to solve a complex problem, generate creative content, or get highly detailed responses, these strategies can aid to the quality and relevance of the results you receive.

### *Step-by-Step Prompts*

The power of step-by-step prompts lies in their ability to guide the language model through a multi-faceted problem in a systematic way. Much like how you might explain a complex process to a friend, breaking down your instructions into manageable parts makes it easier for the model to follow along and provide the most coherent response possible. By segmenting the information, the model can focus on one aspect at a time, leading to more thorough and accurate results.

## The Value of Breaking Down Complexity

The idea behind step-by-step prompts is simple: if the task you have in mind involves multiple parts or stages, prompting the model to respond to each part in turn helps ensure that nothing gets lost or overlooked. Imagine asking someone to explain how to bake a cake, but leaving it at that—you might end up with a broad overview of general instructions. However, if you ask about each part of the process, step by step, you'll get a clear, structured response.

Consider a prompt like, "Explain how to bake a chocolate cake." Instead, by transforming this into a step-by-step instruction, you could say:

1. "List the ingredients needed to bake a chocolate cake."
2. "Describe how to mix the dry ingredients."
3. "Explain how to prepare the wet ingredients."
4. "Guide me through combining both dry and wet ingredients."
5. "Detail the baking process, including oven temperature and timing."

By using this approach, the language model is better equipped to provide precise and thorough responses, capturing every stage of the process. Each step acts as a guidepost, ensuring that the response is complete and logically organized.

## Real-World Examples of Step-by-Step Prompts

Step-by-step prompting is particularly useful in situations that demand logical progression or structured solutions, such as:

- Mathematics and Problem Solving: Instead of asking, "Solve this equation," you could prompt the model step by step: "First, simplify the left side of the equation. Next, isolate the variable. Finally, provide the solution." This method helps to avoid any skipped steps or assumptions and makes it easier to follow the entire solving process.
- Coding and Technical Guidance: When requesting help with coding, instead of asking, "Write a program that sorts an array", break it down: "Step 1: Define the function. Step 2: Outline the sorting logic. Step 3: Implement the sorting algorithm." This can help ensure that each part of the code is logically sound and easy to understand, especially for beginners who need to follow the reasoning behind each line.
- Learning a New Concept: For learning about something new, like "Explain how photosynthesis works", you can structure it: "First, explain what chlorophyll is. Then, describe the role of sunlight. Finally, show how these elements work together to produce energy." This breakdown helps to make sure that no essential part of the explanation is missed, leading to a fuller understanding of the concept.

**Why Step-by-Step Works**

Breaking down tasks into smaller, digestible steps helps the language model to focus on specific aspects without being overwhelmed by complexity. It also minimizes ambiguity, which is often the root cause of confusing or incomplete responses. Just as humans can find large, complex instructions overwhelming, language models benefit from bite-sized prompts that tackle each part of a challenge individually. This process allows the model to deliver more consistent, accurate, and informative outputs.

Moreover, step-by-step prompts help in identifying where potential misunderstandings may arise. If the response to a particular step is incorrect or unclear, you can easily refine that part without having to rework the entire prompt. This iterative process is extremely helpful in achieving a high level of precision and usefulness in the model's output.

The beauty of step-by-step prompts lies in their adaptability—whether you're aiming to solve an intricate math problem, write a detailed report, or understand a multi-step process, guiding the model with incremental prompts results in clearer, more actionable responses. Additionally, this approach can be used for collaborative tasks, where multiple users might be contributing different parts of a larger project. By organizing prompts step by step, everyone involved can follow the logical flow and ensure consistency throughout.

**Humor and Lightness in Step-by-Step**

Let's be honest—breaking things down is not just about effectiveness; it can also make things a bit more fun! Rather than getting a dry, all-in-one answer, you get to have a conversation with the AI, which can add a more interactive and enjoyable dimension to your work. Imagine asking the model to explain "how to deal with a dragon," step-by-step: "Step 1: Assess if it's friendly. Step 2: If not, locate fire-resistant gear." The results can be both informative and entertaining!

This kind of playful engagement can make even mundane or daunting tasks feel lighter. Whether you are working through a serious problem or just exploring creative scenarios, breaking it down into steps can transform the interaction into an engaging back-and-forth exchange. It invites the model to add color to its responses, potentially including humor or creative elements that make the process more enjoyable while still staying on track. So next time you want to add a little spark to

your work, remember that step-by-step prompts are not just practical—
they can also be part of a good storytelling adventure.

## Example-Driven Prompts

Example-driven prompts are a powerful way to shape the output of a
language model by providing clear examples that the model can follow.
This technique leverages the model's ability to recognize patterns and
extrapolate from the information it has been given, allowing you to
guide its responses more effectively and produce high-quality content.

### Why Examples Matter

Using examples within your prompts can dramatically improve the
quality and relevance of the output. When you provide the model with
an example, it helps establish expectations for the kind of response you
are looking for. The model uses the provided example as a template,
which helps it understand your intent more clearly and produce results
that match your needs. In many ways, examples act like a set of training
wheels for the model, ensuring that it stays on the path you want it to
follow.

For instance, if you are asking the model to write a poem, you could add
an example of a line or two: "Write a poem about the ocean.
Here's a line to inspire you: 'The waves dance and twirl in the
golden sun.'" This example helps set the tone, rhythm, and imagery
you want in the poem, guiding the model to produce a response in the
same style.

Examples are particularly useful in creative writing, problem-solving,
and even in answering questions that require a specific format.

Providing examples can reduce ambiguity, making the model's job easier and improving the accuracy of the output.

**Practical Use Cases for Example-Driven Prompts**

- Creative Writing: Suppose you want the model to write a story about a brave knight. Instead of just stating, "Write a story about a brave knight," you could add: "The brave knight, Sir Lancelot, ventured into the dark forest, his armor gleaming under the moonlight." This not only gives the model a character to focus on but also sets the atmosphere and descriptive style you want it to emulate.
- Technical Instructions: If you need technical documentation, an example-driven prompt can be extremely helpful. For instance, if you want the model to explain how to use a specific software tool, you might provide an example like: "When using Tool X, start by opening the dashboard and selecting 'New Project' from the menu." This shows the format and level of detail you are expecting in the response.
- Customer Support Scenarios: In customer service or FAQ generation, examples can ensure that the tone and approach are appropriate. If you want the model to generate responses to common customer questions, you could provide an example like: "If a customer asks how to reset their password, respond with: 'To reset your password, click on the "Forgot Password" link on the login page and follow the instructions sent to your email.'" This helps the model maintain a friendly and helpful tone.

**Crafting Effective Example-Driven Prompts**

To make the most of example-driven prompts, it's essential to provide examples that are as close as possible to what you want in the final output. Be specific, and use examples that reflect the tone, structure, and detail you're aiming for. The more tailored your examples are, the better the model will be able to match them.

It's also helpful to include multiple examples if the prompt is complex or if there are several ways the model could interpret your request. For instance, if you want a model to generate a list of benefits of exercise, you might include examples like: "One benefit of regular exercise is improved cardiovascular health. Another benefit is enhanced mental well-being, as exercise releases endorphins that help reduce stress." By providing more than one example, you help the model understand that you're looking for a list format and that each item should be detailed.

Examples act as powerful guiding tools for AI models, bridging the gap between your expectations and the model's understanding. Whether you're looking for precision, creativity, or a specific response style, well-crafted examples can significantly enhance the quality of the output.

**Balancing Specificity and Flexibility**

One of the challenges with example-driven prompts is finding the right balance between specificity and flexibility. If your example is too rigid or specific, the model might produce something that feels like a copy rather than an original creation inspired by the example. On the other hand, if the example is too vague, it may not provide enough guidance.

For instance, if you're asking the model to write a motivational quote and you give the example: "Believe in yourself, and you can achieve anything," the model may produce similar motivational content but could risk sounding clichéd. To keep it fresh, you might say: "Write a motivational quote that encourages someone to overcome challenges, similar in spirit to: 'Believe in yourself, and you can achieve anything,' but with a unique perspective.". This prompt encourages creativity while still providing a clear framework.

Another approach is to combine several different examples that illustrate a range of possibilities. For example, if you're asking for a story with a plot twist, you could provide multiple mini-stories with twists, each showcasing a different type of surprise or plot development. This encourages the model to innovate while adhering to the spirit of what you're looking for.

Balancing specificity and flexibility ensures that the model has enough direction to stay on track while still allowing room for creative interpretation. It's this balance that often leads to the most satisfying and effective outputs, making example-driven prompting an invaluable technique in your toolkit.

## *Using Output Primers*

Output primers are another effective tool when working with large language models, providing an introductory snippet that sets the tone, context, or direction for the desired output. By including a primer, you give the model a head start, guiding it toward a particular direction without having to provide every detail explicitly. Think of output primers as a springboard—they give the model momentum, nudging it into the intended trajectory from the start.

Using output primers is akin to starting a conversation where you provide the opening lines, and the model picks up from there. This helps maintain consistency in voice, theme, and structure, particularly in longer pieces of text or tasks involving creativity. An effective primer can help ensure the response is aligned with your expectations from the very beginning, minimizing the need for re-dos or significant edits. By giving the model a clear direction, output primers help prevent deviations and keep the response focused, ensuring a higher quality output that meets your needs.

## Why Use Output Primers?

Output primers are invaluable when precision and consistency are crucial, particularly in situations where the tone or depth of information matters. If you're asking the model to produce an article, the primer might include the first few sentences, establishing the voice, rhythm, and subject matter. Similarly, if you're generating a creative story, the primer might introduce the setting or a key character, providing the model with a defined point from which to build. This starting point serves as an anchor, allowing the model to maintain a consistent narrative flow without veering off course.

For instance, consider the prompt: "Write an article about the importance of sleep for mental health." Without additional context, the model might choose a particular style or focus area that doesn't align with your needs. By adding a primer such as, "Sleep is one of the foundational pillars of mental well-being, playing a critical role in cognitive function, emotional regulation, and overall health. In today's fast-paced world, getting adequate rest can often seem like a luxury, yet it is essential," you establish a clear direction for the content. The model then continues with that established tone and perspective, ensuring a more cohesive and tailored response.

In creative contexts, primers work well to spark imagination while ensuring the narrative stays on track. Imagine prompting the model to complete a story with the primer: "In a kingdom far beyond the mountains, there lived a young prince who had never seen the stars, until one night when..." This starting point gives the
50

model a narrative context, and it encourages storytelling that matches the setting and tone. The model is able to pick up from this initial spark and build a story that feels natural and consistent with your original vision.

## Practical Examples of Output Primers

- Formal Reports: Suppose you need a formal report discussing climate change. Instead of simply stating, "Write a report on climate change," include a primer like: "Climate change represents one of the greatest challenges of the 21st century, affecting ecosystems, economies, and communities worldwide. This report will explore the key drivers, impacts, and mitigation strategies." This not only sets the scene but also conveys the structure and formality you are expecting. The model is guided to follow a specific path, resulting in a well-organized and comprehensive response.
- Creative Stories: When crafting creative stories, primers help the model understand your vision. For example, "The garden had always been a sanctuary for Elena, a place where she could escape the noise of the city. But today, something felt different—a strange whisper carried through the leaves, drawing her deeper into the unknown." Such primers give the model context, setting, and a spark of intrigue to build on, ensuring a cohesive continuation. The result is a story that maintains the mood and direction you had in mind, with a smooth flow from the primer to the continuation.
- Emails and Correspondence: Output primers can be particularly useful for emails. Instead of saying, "Write an email to apologize for a late response", you could begin with a primer: "Dear [Name], I hope this message finds you

well. I wanted to reach out and apologize for the delay in my response." This primer gives the model a polished opening that can then be expanded appropriately, ensuring that the tone remains courteous and professional throughout the email.

## Crafting Effective Output Primers

The key to crafting effective primers is to establish a clear tone, style, and level of detail. A good primer should:

1. Set the Scene: Introduce the subject matter or character to provide context. For a factual report, provide background details; for creative writing, establish the setting. This helps the model understand the focus and context, ensuring that the response starts off strong and relevant.
2. Reflect the Desired Tone: If you need a formal response, the primer should use formal language. If it's meant to be light and humorous, the primer should set that playful tone. The primer acts as a tone-setter, helping the model to match the desired style right from the beginning.
3. Guide Structure: Establish how the response should be organized. For instance, if you're writing an argumentative piece, the primer might introduce the main argument and hint at the subsequent structure. This structural guidance helps the model generate content that is logical and well-organized, reducing the need for significant edits later.

The more nuanced the primer, the more effectively it can guide the model's output. However, it's important to leave enough space for creativity—don't over-constrain the model. The primer should serve as a catalyst, not a complete roadmap. The goal is to set the stage and let the model take it from there, allowing for a natural and dynamic continuation.

## Balancing Guidance with Flexibility

The effectiveness of output primers also lies in finding the right balance between giving enough direction and allowing flexibility. If the primer is overly prescriptive, the resulting text may feel stilted or limited. On the other hand, too vague a primer may lead to content that strays from your original intention. Striking the right balance ensures that the model has a clear path while still allowing for organic and engaging content.

For example, rather than starting a story with, "Once upon a time, a princess named Clara lived in a castle. She was unhappy because..." which locks the narrative into a particular conflict, you could broaden it slightly: "Once upon a time, a princess named Clara lived in a castle where things were not always as they seemed." This provides intrigue and direction while still giving the model room to explore different narrative possibilities. By maintaining an element of mystery, you allow the model to inject creativity while staying aligned with your vision.

In sum, output primers are a fantastic way to shape and refine the model's output. Whether you're aiming for creativity, factual accuracy, or formal correspondence, the primer serves as the starting line, ensuring that the model takes off in the right direction and delivers content that meets your needs. By mastering the use of output primers, you can add consistency, relevance, and creativity to the AI-generated content, making your prompts more effective and your interactions more satisfying. Primers help bridge the gap between your expectations and the model's capabilities, making the process smoother, more predictable, and ultimately more rewarding.

# FIVE

## Managing Model Behavior

Successfully managing the behavior of large language models can be likened to parenting an immensely knowledgeable yet unpredictable child. These models have the power to assist in countless areas, but they can also exhibit biases, misunderstand human cues, or even go off on tangents if not guided properly. This chapter is dedicated to understanding how we can take charge of an LLM's output, nudging it in the right direction to ensure it behaves appropriately, helps meaningfully, and ultimately adds value to our interaction. Whether you are managing potential biases, seeking responses that sound naturally human, or guiding the model to take on a specific persona or role, these techniques will help you shape your model's behavior in an intentional way.

## *Bias Control*

Bias is an unavoidable phenomenon, not just in human beings, but also in machine learning models. Bias in language models arises because of the data these models are trained on, which inevitably reflects the biases present in human texts and media. While some biases are harmless, others can skew the model's responses in unintended ways, leading to potential misinformation, stereotypes, or inequitable outputs. Hence, bias control becomes one of the critical aspects of managing model behavior.

To mitigate bias, the first step is to understand that language models mirror their training data. If we can be mindful of the prompts we provide, we can actively steer the model towards more balanced and fair responses. A practical way to do this is by specifying that the model's answer should be impartial or to request it to consider multiple perspectives.

For instance, consider asking the model: "Describe the pros and cons of remote work. Ensure that your answer reflects diverse viewpoints, including both employees and employers from various backgrounds." This kind of prompt encourages the model to avoid giving a one-sided response. By explicitly telling the model to consider different perspectives, we minimize the risk of biased output.

Another effective technique for bias control is called "Reinforcement via Redirection"—if you notice a biased or inappropriate response, provide constructive feedback and guide the model toward a different direction. For example, if the model provides an answer that leans too heavily on a particular stereotype, you can prompt it to "reconsider the answer without relying on stereotypes." Encouraging the model to revisit its output with clear instructions can lead to more responsible, balanced responses.

Moreover, using prompts like "Explain this concept while avoiding gender stereotypes" or "Provide an unbiased overview of the issue" works well in encouraging fairness in its replies. Training yourself to recognize subtle biases in responses and immediately addressing them with follow-up prompts is crucial to maintaining high-quality, ethically sound interactions.

Bias control is not a one-time action; it requires vigilance and iterative effort. If a response still carries unintended biases, don't hesitate to correct the model and try again. With each iteration, the responses can become more aligned with fairness, reducing the impact of the inherent biases present in the training data.

**Example Prompt for Bias Control:**

- "Summarize the benefits of early childhood education, making sure not to express gender-biased stereotypes about which children benefit more."

Controlling bias requires patience and proactive management, but it ensures that the information you receive is not only accurate but also equitable and just. When used effectively, bias control can make interactions with language models more reliable, ensuring that outputs serve diverse audiences in fair and respectful ways.

## *Encouraging Human-like Responses*

One of the most fascinating abilities of language models is their capability to generate text that mimics human communication. However, left to its own devices, a model may produce content that's either too mechanical or doesn't quite capture the nuances of human interaction. Encouraging human-like responses is about crafting prompts that lead the model to offer replies that sound relatable, empathetic, and conversational.

To get human-like responses, you need to provide explicit instructions within your prompt. For example, instead of simply asking, "Explain what meditation is," you could say, "Explain what meditation is in a friendly, conversational tone, as if you're chatting with a friend who's new to it." Adding phrases like 'in a friendly tone' or 'in simple, everyday language' gives the model additional cues to shape its response in a more accessible manner.

Another strategy is to give the model a role that inherently invites warmth and empathy. For instance, "You are a comforting friend explaining how to handle stress to someone who's feeling overwhelmed." Such prompts prompt the model to add layers of empathy and reassurance that would come naturally in a human-to-human conversation.

Consider using analogies and storytelling to further enhance the human-like feel of the response. Language models can produce beautiful analogies when prompted well. For example, instead of asking, "Describe how photosynthesis works," you could prompt, "Describe how photosynthesis works as if you're telling a story about a leaf's journey to gather sunlight and make food." This not only makes the explanation more engaging but also feels more like a natural conversation.

Another useful approach is to ask the model to draw on relatable everyday experiences. For instance, instead of asking, "Explain the benefits of regular exercise," you could say, "Explain the benefits of regular exercise by comparing it to maintaining a car—just like how a car needs regular maintenance, our bodies need consistent movement to stay in good shape." By inviting the model to use familiar comparisons, you make the response more tangible and relatable to the reader.

**Example Prompt for Human-like Responses:**

- "Describe the benefits of regular exercise in an encouraging way, as if you're motivating a friend who's thinking about getting back into fitness."

The aim is to bridge the gap between AI and human communication, ensuring that responses resonate more deeply with the user by being relatable, warm, and engaging. Achieving this level of conversational authenticity may require some fine-tuning, but the payoff is well worth it when you receive answers that feel genuinely helpful and personal.

## Role Assignment

Role assignment is a powerful tool that allows you to specify exactly how you want the model to behave during an interaction. This technique is particularly helpful in situations where specialized knowledge or a particular tone is needed. By assigning a role, you are giving the model a persona, allowing it to better align its output with your expectations.

Roles can be as varied as the tasks at hand. For example, if you want detailed financial advice, you can tell the model: "You are a seasoned financial advisor. Provide a comprehensive plan for someone looking to start investing with a modest budget." This framing provides the context the model needs to respond in a more informed and expert manner.

Role assignment is also incredibly effective for creative endeavors. If you are working on a piece of fiction, you could ask the model to take on the role of a "creative writing coach" or even a 'character in your story' to help brainstorm dialogue or plot twists. For example, "You are a detective in a noir mystery. Narrate the scene as you walk into a dimly lit room filled with clues." These kinds of prompts immerse the model in a specific persona, which leads to outputs rich in detail and closely aligned with the context you envision.

Roles can also be used for educational purposes. If you are learning about a technical topic, you might assign the model the role of a "teacher for beginners," ensuring the explanations are simple and easy to digest. For instance, "You are a high school physics teacher. Explain Newton's third law in a way that a teenager could easily understand." By clarifying the role, the model tailors its responses to meet the expected knowledge level and tone.

Another way to leverage role assignment is by using the model as a collaborator for brainstorming sessions. For example, "You are a creative marketing specialist. Help me brainstorm ideas for a campaign to promote a new eco-friendly product." Here, you are directing the model to take on a specific mindset, which can lead to more targeted and imaginative suggestions.

**Example Prompt for Role Assignment:**

- "You are a career counselor. Give me advice on how to transition from a career in retail to one in digital marketing, emphasizing practical first steps."

By assigning roles, you are effectively setting boundaries and expectations, guiding the model to respond in the way that is most beneficial to your particular needs and circumstances. The more detailed you are with assigning roles, the more accurately the model can meet your specific requirements, leading to richer and more useful outputs.

# SIX

## Advanced Techniques for Complex Tasks

When basic prompting approaches aren't enough, it's time to call upon the advanced arsenal. These advanced techniques are particularly useful when you need the model to navigate more complex instructions, interpret subtle nuances, or generate responses that require in-depth analysis. By employing these methods, you can elevate your interactions and make the most out of the model's capabilities, achieving richer, more detailed, and precise outputs. Let's delve into some of the most powerful strategies that can elevate your AI interactions to the next level, providing greater depth and insight.

### *Chain-of-Thought (CoT) Prompting*

Chain-of-Thought (CoT) prompting is an advanced approach that aims to make the model think step-by-step before arriving at the final answer. Instead of prompting the model to provide an immediate, one-off response, CoT prompts guide it to break down complex questions into manageable segments, fostering logical progression and deeper analysis. This technique mirrors how humans often tackle difficult problems—by breaking them into smaller, more digestible parts that are easier to understand and solve.

Imagine you're trying to solve a complicated math problem or a riddle. Instead of immediately trying to find the answer, you'd likely jot down intermediate steps, allowing each solution to guide you to the next. Chain-of-Thought prompting harnesses the same idea but in the context of LLM interactions. By asking the model to provide intermediate reasoning, we can nudge it toward more coherent and well-supported conclusions, enhancing both accuracy and detail while reducing the risk of errors.

The benefits of Chain-of-Thought prompting are substantial. By encouraging the model to walk through the problem incrementally, you can effectively minimize logical leaps and ensure that no crucial steps are overlooked. This is especially valuable for complex, layered tasks where each step builds upon the previous one, requiring meticulous thought progression. CoT prompting can also help reveal the reasoning behind the model's output, making it easier for users to follow along and understand the solution process.

**Example of Chain-of-Thought Prompting**

Consider a scenario where you need the model to solve a logic puzzle:

**Prompt:**

"A farmer has three animals—a cow, a goat, and a chicken. The farmer needs to cross a river but can only carry one animal at a time. The goat will eat the chicken if left alone, and the cow might wander off. How does the farmer get all three across the river without any issues? Think ahead step-by-step and then come up with your answer."

With Chain-of-Thought prompting, the model will eventually generate reasoning similar to:

1. The farmer takes the goat across first.

2. Then, the farmer goes back and takes the chicken across, leaving it on the opposite side while taking the goat back.

3. The farmer then takes the cow across.

4. Finally, the farmer returns for the goat.

This structured process allows the model to break down the solution step-by-step, ensuring accuracy and coherence.

Using CoT prompting is particularly effective in domains such as:

- Mathematics: Solving multi-step problems, where each calculation or decision influences the next. By breaking down the problem, the model ensures no crucial calculation is skipped.

- Reasoning: Complex decision-making scenarios, where evaluating each factor separately leads to a more balanced decision. CoT helps in laying out each factor clearly, leading to a more well-rounded output.

- Science: Breaking down experimental processes or explaining concepts progressively, allowing for clarity in each stage. CoT can ensure that each stage of an experiment is described in detail, avoiding oversimplification or misunderstanding.

One crucial tip for successful Chain-of-Thought prompting is to explicitly include terms like "think ahead step-by-step" or "let's solve this in stages" in your prompt. This helps nudge the model toward a more logical and systematic path, avoiding common pitfalls of rushing to conclusions or missing important steps. It also makes the response more educational and informative, helping users learn not just the answer but the process as well.

## Automatic Chain-of-Thought (Auto-CoT)

Automatic Chain-of-Thought (Auto-CoT) is the next evolutionary step from standard Chain-of-Thought prompting. While the original CoT technique often requires careful crafting of intermediate reasoning paths by the user, Auto-CoT allows the (modern and capable) model itself to generate these intermediate steps autonomously, making it an even more efficient tool for tackling complex queries without needing the user to explicitly guide each step. Note that not every model out there has been given the ability to do Auto-CoT.

In essence, Auto-CoT automates the process of prompting the model to engage in a detailed thought process. It essentially asks the model, "Hey, let's walk through this one step at a time," but without requiring the user to manually script out each phase of the thought progression. This is ideal when you need detailed analysis but don't have the time or expertise to outline every stage of the reasoning journey. It allows for a more seamless interaction while still achieving detailed, step-by-step results. With Auto-CoT, the model actively generates its own intermediate reasoning, which not only saves time but also leads to more dynamic and adaptive responses. This approach is particularly beneficial when facing problems that can have multiple pathways to a solution, as the model is encouraged to explore various potential steps before deciding on the best route. The flexibility of Auto-CoT makes it well-suited for a wide range of tasks, from technical explanations to creative problem-solving. Auto-CoT works particularly well when combined with clear instructions, such as specifying that the model should adopt a systematic, stepwise approach. By doing so, the model is empowered to autonomously decide the steps that make the most logical sense, allowing for adaptive, contextually appropriate responses. This is particularly useful in cases where the pathway to the solution might vary depending on the nuances of the input provided. It allows the model to be more explorative, enhancing both the depth and breadth of its analysis.

**Example of Auto-CoT in Practice**

Suppose you need an answer to a nuanced question like:

**Prompt:**

"Explain how renewable energy sources can collectively contribute to reducing global carbon emissions. Walk through each source step-by-step."

The model might autonomously generate:

1. Solar Energy: Discusses the reduction in carbon emissions due to decreased reliance on fossil fuels, as well as the scalability of solar panels in both residential and industrial contexts. It also touches on advancements in solar technology that have made it more efficient and cost-effective.

2. Wind Energy: Explains how wind turbines can replace coal and gas power plants, highlighting their impact on local and national grids. The model might also explore the potential challenges, such as variability in wind patterns and solutions like energy storage systems.

3. Hydropower: Analyzes the role of hydroelectric dams in providing a stable and renewable energy source that can replace carbon-intensive power. It may also discuss the environmental considerations associated with large dams and how modern designs are mitigating these impacts.

4. Geothermal Energy: Explains how harnessing geothermal energy can provide a consistent power source with minimal emissions, especially in

64

regions with active geothermal features. The model may also elaborate on the scalability and regional limitations of geothermal energy.

Auto-CoT shines in situations where in-depth exploration of topics is required, such as educational contexts, complex scientific explanations, and legal analysis. The model, equipped with the right instructions, will autonomously create a structured breakdown, making it easier for the reader to follow along. It encourages the model to "think out loud," providing a window into its reasoning process, which can be particularly informative and enlightening for users who want more than just the final answer.

One caution with Auto-CoT is that it requires the right balance between providing structure and giving the model enough freedom to think for itself. If the prompt is overly restrictive, the model may not fully leverage its ability to develop the solution autonomously, thereby reducing the effectiveness of this technique. On the other hand, giving the model too much freedom without enough context can lead to wandering responses that lack focus.

**NOTE**

*Auto-CoT is not a tool or extension you install, but rather a prompting technique that utilizes the inherent reasoning abilities of large language models (LLMs). It works by allowing the model to generate intermediate reasoning steps automatically, enhancing the quality of its outputs for tasks that require logical or multi-step reasoning. The technique relies entirely on how you frame your prompts implicitly to generate reasoning chains without explicit step-by-step guidance or examples.*

**Comparison of CoT and Auto-CoT**

| Feature | Chain-of-Thought (CoT) | Automatic Chain-of-Thought (Auto-CoT) |
|---------|------------------------|----------------------------------------|
| Guidance in Prompt | Explicit examples/templates provided | No explicit examples; model infers reasoning |
| Ease of Use | Requires crafting detailed prompts | Simpler prompts, model does the heavy lifting |
| Flexibility | Better for specific or custom reasoning | Ideal for general and adaptive reasoning tasks |
| When to Use | When step-by-step logic must be taught | When the task naturally involves logical steps |

*Note.* The difference between Chain-of-Thought (CoT) and Automatic Chain-of-Thought (Auto-CoT) lies in how reasoning chains are generated and their level of explicit guidance.

## Self-Consistency

Self-Consistency is a relatively new but highly impactful approach that focuses on boosting the reliability of the model's outputs. In the context of LLMs, self-consistency involves generating multiple reasoning chains and cross-verifying them to identify the most consistent answer. Rather than relying on a single chain of thought, the model is prompted to explore multiple pathways to a solution, increasing the likelihood of reaching an accurate and well-supported conclusion.

Imagine having multiple attempts at solving a complex problem and then comparing those attempts to determine the answer that appears the most frequently or is backed by the most consistent logic. Self-

Consistency is about using this principle to filter out spurious or incorrect responses and select the one that aligns best with common sense and logic. This not only increases accuracy but also provides a level of reliability that single-shot responses may lack.

By generating multiple reasoning chains, the model can compare different solutions, effectively cross-referencing its own work. This technique is invaluable when tackling ambiguous questions, where there may not be a single clear answer. Instead of depending on one attempt, the model evaluates several possibilities, improving the chances that the final output is both correct and comprehensive. Self-Consistency also helps to mitigate biases that might arise from any single reasoning path, leading to more balanced and nuanced outputs.

**Example of Self-Consistency**

Consider a complex problem involving causal reasoning:

**Prompt:**

"A company has experienced declining sales for the past three quarters. Describe three possible causes for this decline and suggest the most likely one."

Instead of immediately providing a single reasoning path, the model may produce multiple iterations, such as:

- Chain 1: Declining product quality leading to customer dissatisfaction. This chain might explore specific feedback from customers and highlight common complaints.

- Chain 2: Increased competition in the market reducing the company's market share. The model could elaborate on new competitors, their pricing strategies, and market shifts that have impacted the company.

- Chain 3: Ineffective marketing campaigns failing to reach the target audience. This chain might discuss metrics such as decreased engagement rates and a lack of targeted outreach.

Once these chains are produced, the model then evaluates which reasoning appears the most frequently across iterations or is best supported by the provided context. The final answer might reflect the most consistent reasoning, such as "Increased competition in the market," because it showed up in the majority of reasoning chains and aligned with available data.

Self-Consistency is particularly beneficial when there is a high potential for ambiguity, and more than one valid pathway could exist. By generating multiple thought processes and cross-referencing them, the model essentially self-verifies, thereby reducing the chances of a misleading or incorrect response. This approach is also helpful in providing transparency, as users can see the various reasoning paths the model explored before arriving at a conclusion.

To employ it effectively, it's essential to prompt the model with something like: "Generate multiple solutions and select the one with the most consistent reasoning." This ensures the model doesn't simply settle for the first response but rather checks itself to enhance reliability and coherence. The process of self-verification adds an extra layer of scrutiny, making the final output more dependable.

This approach can be especially effective in creative domains as well, such as story generation, where multiple narrative paths could lead to equally compelling outcomes. By generating several storylines and evaluating them for consistency, the model can produce a final version that captures the most engaging and coherent elements from each. This technique not only improves accuracy but also enhances creativity by allowing multiple ideas to be explored before settling on the best one.

## Conclusion

These advanced techniques—Chain-of-Thought prompting, Automatic Chain-of-Thought, and Self-Consistency—represent some of the most powerful ways to manage the model's behavior for more complex and intricate tasks. Whether you need detailed step-by-step reasoning, automated pathways through nuanced content, or cross-verified consistency, these methods give you the ability to coax the best possible performance out of your LLM interactions.

Advanced prompting isn't just about asking better questions; it's about understanding how the model processes those questions and guiding it toward deeper, more reliable outputs. With these tools, you can make LLMs tackle even the most challenging queries with precision and thoroughness, helping you achieve results that are not only accurate but insightful and well-structured. The key to success lies in experimentation and adaptation. By familiarizing yourself with these advanced techniques, you can learn when and how to apply them effectively, enhancing the quality of interactions and ensuring that your prompts yield the most meaningful and informative results possible. Whether you're solving mathematical puzzles, analyzing complex scenarios, or creating richly detailed narratives, these strategies will empower you to make the most of what advanced language models have to offer.

Remember, advanced prompting techniques are iterative—each interaction provides insights that can help you refine your approach, making your future prompts even more powerful. By mastering these methods, you can transform your AI interactions into a highly effective tool for problem-solving, creative thinking, and deep analysis, pushing the limits of what's possible with language models.

# SEVEN

## Optimizing for Creative and Technical Tasks

With a little fine-tuning, language models can excel at both creative and highly technical tasks. Adjusting how we prompt and interact with them can make a significant difference in the quality of the outputs, whether we're writing poetry or generating clean, functional code. In this chapter, we'll explore various ways to optimize your prompts to better match the demands of creative and technical domains. We'll start with adjusting temperature to control creativity, then move on to methods for controlling response length, and conclude with techniques for managing code and other technical outputs. Each section will provide practical examples, detailed guidance, and tips for maximizing the model's performance across different scenarios.

### *Adjusting Temperature for Creativity*

In the world of prompting, "temperature" is an incredibly powerful setting that allows you to influence the nature of the responses generated by a language model. In this context, temperature is a parameter that determines how deterministic or random the model's outputs will be. A lower temperature yields more predictable responses, while a higher temperature produces more varied and imaginative ones. Adjusting temperature is particularly useful when you want to foster creativity or control how "adventurous" the model's responses are.

Think of temperature like a dial on a creative thermostat. When you need practical, straightforward answers, set the temperature lower. When you need fresh, innovative ideas—like a new twist on an old story, a brainstorming session, or an unconventional piece of art—you can crank the temperature up. Let's explore this idea a bit further with examples and specific applications, highlighting how adjusting this parameter can unlock different capabilities of the model.

**Low vs. High Temperature: Practical Application**

Imagine you're working on two different projects. One involves writing technical documentation, and the other involves crafting a fictional storyline for a sci-fi universe. For the technical documentation, you want clarity and accuracy, so you set the temperature low. The model focuses on well-known facts and delivers outputs that are coherent, predictable, and to the point.

**Prompt with Low Temperature:**

"Explain how solar panels convert sunlight into electricity in clear, simple terms."

Output with Low Temperature: "Solar panels convert sunlight into electricity using photovoltaic cells, which capture solar energy and transform it into electrical current through the photoelectric effect. The electricity is then converted from direct current (DC) to alternating current (AC) using an inverter, making it suitable for household or commercial use."

In this case, a low temperature keeps the explanation straightforward and factual, avoiding unnecessary detours or creative interpretations that could cloud the explanation.

On the other hand, when you're brainstorming for a sci-fi universe, you might want something less predictable—something that sparks your imagination and breaks away from conventional tropes. This is where a high temperature comes into play.

72

**Prompt with High Temperature:**

"Create a backstory for an intergalactic traveler who encounters an unexpected civilization on a distant planet."

Output with High Temperature: "Drifting through the outer fringes of the Andromeda galaxy, Captain Elara stumbled upon an iridescent world shimmering like a fractured diamond in space. Upon landing, she found that its inhabitants communicated not through words, but through vivid, pulsating patterns on their skin—a complex language of light that held the secrets of an ancient alliance between stars, unseen by any human eyes before. They spoke of a forgotten treaty with a race made of pure energy that protected the solar tides, and soon Elara found herself tasked with renewing the pact to save her own universe."

By setting the temperature setting or the (tone-)temperature withing the prompt itself higher, you get a more unpredictable, dynamic output that adds texture and depth to the creative narrative. The details are unexpected, rich, and can inspire further ideas—ideal for storytelling, brainstorming, or conceptual art. This approach can be particularly useful for writers, content creators, and marketers looking to inject a burst of originality into their work.

## Practical Scenarios for Adjusting Temperature

- Low Temperature Scenarios: Technical writing, fact-based answers, instruction manuals, academic content, customer service responses. When you need the output to be precise, informative, and devoid of creative embellishments, keeping the temperature low ensures accuracy and reliability.
- High Temperature Scenarios: Creative writing, poetry, brainstorming sessions, marketing taglines, world-building for fiction. These scenarios benefit from unpredictability, originality,

and creative diversity, which a higher temperature setting can easily provide.

When using temperature adjustment effectively, it's often a good idea to experiment with different values, if your model supports input fields for temperature settings. Temperature can be adjusted along a scale typically ranging from 0 to 1.0. For most practical applications, a temperature of around 0.2 to 0.4 works well for more factual and straightforward content. Meanwhile, a setting of 0.7 to 1.0 is best for fostering creativity and spontaneity. It's also worth noting that these values aren't fixed—different projects may require subtle tweaks to find the sweet spot.

The key is to understand the balance between creativity and coherence. Lower temperatures minimize the model's exploratory tendencies, helping it stay closer to what's already known or established. High temperatures amplify the model's ability to generate novel, surprising, and sometimes whimsical content, but it comes with a risk of reduced consistency and factual accuracy. This trade-off is important to consider, especially in contexts where factual correctness is crucial.

When working on projects that benefit from a touch of both—such as educational content that also needs to engage—try a medium setting (e.g., 0.5) that allows some creative latitude while retaining a solid grounding in facts. It's this nuanced control that allows you to tailor the outputs to fit the exact nature of the task at hand, optimizing both productivity and quality of the results. For example, creating an engaging explainer video script might benefit from a medium temperature setting to ensure the content is both informative and captivating.

Another interesting application of temperature settings involves fine-tuning prompts to match different audiences. For instance, when addressing younger audiences, a slightly higher temperature can make the content more colorful and engaging, whereas a more conservative temperature might be better suited for business reports or legal documentation. The flexibility to adjust the level of creativity allows you to cater your outputs to different target audiences, ensuring the response is always appropriate and impactful.

In summary, adjusting the temperature is like tuning the personality of the model's responses. Low temperatures produce fact-based, reliable content, perfect for technical or academic work, while high temperatures yield imaginative, diverse, and sometimes surprising outputs, ideal for creative projects. By experimenting with these settings, you can harness the model's full potential, whether your aim is to inform, entertain, or inspire.

**NOTE**

Explicit settings (e.g., GPT APIs, Playgrounds) allow control over output creativity: low values (e.g., 0.2) for focused, precise answers; high values (e.g., 0.8) for creative, varied responses. In interfaces without settings (e.g., ChatGPT browser), adjust by crafting precise prompts for deterministic outputs or open-ended ones for creativity.

## Controlling Response Length

When crafting prompts, one essential factor to consider is the desired length of the output. Different tasks require different levels of detail— sometimes you need a brief summary, while other times a comprehensive, in-depth response is necessary. Controlling the length(-setting) of the response can help align the output with your specific needs, whether for concise information or for expanded, creative exploration. This flexibility allows you to achieve the right balance between brevity and detail, ensuring that the generated content is fit for purpose.

## Why Length Control Matters

The length of an LLM's response can significantly impact the quality and usability of the generated content. For instance, generating a succinct answer might be crucial when summarizing key points or drafting content that needs to be quickly digestible. Conversely, longer, more detailed responses can provide depth, context, and elaboration that is invaluable for research, storytelling, or complex problem-solving.

Consider a situation where you need a quick overview of a topic like renewable energy. A concise response helps you get the essence without unnecessary elaboration. However, if you're researching for a report or writing an article, you would prefer a lengthier, detailed output that dives into various facets, such as technologies, advantages, challenges, and future trends. This distinction highlights the importance of tailoring the response length to the specific requirements of the task at hand.

## Techniques for Controlling Response Length

1. Explicitly State the Desired Length: The most straightforward way to control response length is to specify your preference directly within the prompt. Using instructions like "Provide a brief summary of..." or "Write a detailed explanation of..." helps set clear expectations for the model. You can also be more specific by defining the number of sentences or paragraphs you want.

- Example for a short response: "Summarize the key features of machine learning in two sentences."
- Example for a detailed response: "Provide an in-depth explanation of machine learning, covering its definition, types, and applications, in at least five paragraphs."

By explicitly stating the desired length, you eliminate ambiguity and guide the model to generate content that meets your specific requirements, making the output more useful and relevant.

2. Incorporate Length Indicators: You can use words that inherently indicate the level of detail expected, such as "overview," "summary," "detailed analysis," or "comprehensive discussion." These terms can nudge the model to generate responses that fit the desired length and depth.
   - Example: "Give a detailed analysis of the causes and effects of climate change." This will likely result in a longer response compared to simply asking, "What is climate change?"

Length indicators help the model understand the scope of the response, ensuring that it aligns with your expectations regarding detail and complexity.

3. Use Primers or Starters to Set the Tone: Providing a starting point can also be an effective way to manage length. For example, starting a prompt with "In detail, explain how..." sets a tone that the model follows to generate a more elaborate response.

Primers act as a cue for the model, signaling whether a brief or extended answer is required, thereby helping to shape the response appropriately.

4. Chunk the Information: If you need a longer and detailed answer, it might be useful to break the request into smaller chunks or sections. For instance, instead of asking for a broad explanation of quantum computing, you could create a prompt like: "First, explain the basic principles of quantum mechanics. Then, discuss how these principles are applied in quantum computing." This method encourages the model to generate a more organized and extended output.

Chunking information makes it easier for the model to focus on specific parts of a broader topic, resulting in a well-structured and thorough response that covers all necessary aspects without overwhelming the reader.

5. Iteration and Refinement: Length control often involves iterative prompting. If the initial response is either too brief or too elaborate, you can refine the prompt to adjust the output. For example, if the output was too short, you might follow up with: "Can you expand on the challenges involved in this process?" Conversely, if it was too long, you might ask: "Summarize the key points from the previous explanation." This iterative approach helps to fine-tune the length to exactly what you need.

Refinement through iteration allows you to gradually shape the response, ensuring it meets your precise needs in terms of detail and scope.

6. Temperature Settings: Although primarily used for creativity, temperature settings can also indirectly influence length. Higher temperature values lead to more varied and exploratory answers, which can result in longer responses. In contrast, lower temperatures yield more focused and concise outputs.

Adjusting the temperature can be a subtle yet effective way to manage the length and tone of the response, especially when balancing between creative elaboration and focused brevity.

## Practical Example

Imagine you are writing a blog post on the benefits of meditation. If you need a quick snippet for a social media teaser, your prompt might be: "Summarize the benefits of meditation in one or two sentences." The model might respond with: "Meditation helps reduce stress, improves focus, and enhances emotional well-being."

However, for the full blog post, you would want a much deeper exploration: "Write a detailed blog post on the benefits of meditation, including its effects on mental health, physical health, and productivity." The response would then include multiple sections, offering a comprehensive overview of how meditation impacts various aspects of life, complete with examples and explanations.

This example illustrates how controlling response length can help tailor the content to different purposes, from quick, engaging snippets to in-depth explorations.

## Balancing Length and Quality

One common challenge when controlling length is balancing detail with clarity. A long response that meanders without providing valuable information can be as unhelpful as an overly brief answer. To strike the right balance, it's crucial to frame your prompts in a way that encourages both depth and focus.

For instance, instead of simply asking for a detailed explanation, you could specify: "Provide a detailed explanation of photosynthesis, focusing on the role of sunlight, chlorophyll, and carbon dioxide." This way, you guide the model not only on how long the response should be but also on what aspects to focus on, ensuring that the detail provided is both relevant and informative.

By specifying the key elements to cover, you ensure that the response remains focused and does not drift into unrelated topics, thereby maintaining both quality and relevance.

In conclusion, effectively controlling the length of LLM responses is a powerful skill that helps ensure the generated content aligns with your specific needs—whether that means being brief and to the point or offering an in-depth exploration. By using clear instructions, refining prompts iteratively, and providing appropriate context, you can harness the full potential of language models for both concise and comprehensive outputs. This approach not only enhances the quality of the generated content but also makes it more adaptable to a wide range of applications, from quick summaries to detailed reports.

**NOTE**

*Canvas mode in the ChatGPT browser version allows for extended responses by adjusting the context size for singe parts of an output. While it's great for detailed or lengthy outputs, excessively long responses can reduce quality, leading to less focused or repetitive content. For the best balance, keep requests concise and refine outputs incrementally if greater detail is needed.*

## Managing Code and Technical Prompts

When crafting prompts for generating or analyzing code, precision becomes paramount. Technical tasks such as coding require exact details to produce efficient and error-free outputs, and the way you frame your prompt can significantly impact the response quality.

To begin with, managing code prompts often involves providing context and clear requirements. Think of it as giving precise instructions to a junior developer. The model can produce quality code snippets only if it knows exactly what you're looking for. For instance, if you want Python code to solve a specific problem, you should specify the exact requirements—what input the function will take, what output is expected, and any special cases to consider.

Consider an example where you're writing a prompt to generate a script for sorting a list of items in Python. A basic, unclear prompt like "Write code to sort a list" might yield a functional response, but one that's generic and lacking robustness. Instead, consider this more elaborate prompt: "Write a Python function named sort_list that takes a list of integers and returns it in ascending order. Ensure the function includes type checking to handle only integers and raises an error for invalid inputs." By being specific, you significantly increase the likelihood of receiving a response that is both accurate and aligned with your needs.

Another key consideration when managing technical prompts is breaking down complex coding requests. The model works better when each part of the task is presented step-by-step. Instead of asking the model to "Create a web application that tracks user activity", break this down: first ask for code that sets up a basic server, then a function to track user activity, and finally how to integrate this into a web interface. This step-by-step approach not only keeps the outputs more manageable but also helps you identify issues at each stage.

## Providing Context and Dependencies

Context matters greatly in code prompts, especially when dependencies are involved. If you need the generated code to make use of certain libraries or follow specific conventions, mention these explicitly. For example: "Write a Python script to read CSV data using the Pandas library and plot the data using Matplotlib." This ensures the model doesn't simply reinvent the wheel using basic file handling, but utilizes powerful and established libraries that are fit for the task.

Consider providing an example of expected input and output to help guide the model toward the correct approach. For instance, "Write a function that accepts a list of dictionaries representing users, where each dictionary contains name and age fields, and returns a list of names sorted by age. Here's an example input and expected output..." Giving an explicit structure reduces ambiguity and helps the model "see" the kind of logic and structure you desire.

Another powerful technique involves using pseudo-code to guide the model. Suppose you need a complex piece of logic implemented—laying it out in plain language or even pseudo-code can be tremendously helpful: "Write a function that, given a string, returns the frequency of each character. First, initialize an empty dictionary. Then iterate through the string, adding each character to the dictionary if it doesn't exist or updating its count if it does..." By guiding the model in this stepwise manner, it is more likely to arrive at a logical, well-structured response.

## Formatting for Legibility

When managing technical prompts, the formatting of both the prompt and the output is essential for clarity. Use formatting tags or clearly separate sections for input and expected behavior. This practice also extends to managing code outputs that span across multiple files. In such cases, you can provide structured instructions like: "Generate a Python project with two files. The first should contain a function that scrapes web data, and the second should use this function to save data to a local file. Include clear import statements."

Encourage the model to comment its code. Prompts like "Provide detailed comments for each function and explain complex logic sections" can lead to outputs that are much easier to understand, especially for longer or more intricate coding tasks. This is particularly useful when generating code intended for use by others or for your future reference when you might need a refresher on the logic.

## Handling Errors and Edge Cases

Lastly, technical prompts should consider error handling. If you don't mention exceptions or error conditions, the generated code might lack robustness. An effective prompt could be: "Create a function to read a file and return its contents, with proper error handling for cases where the file does not exist or the read operation fails." This way, you ensure that the model includes all the practical considerations that make the code usable in real-world scenarios.

When working on complex tasks, it's also beneficial to think about edge cases that might break the code and include those in your prompt. For instance, if you're writing a prompt for a function that divides two numbers, you could add: "Ensure the function handles division by zero by raising an appropriate error." This approach not only helps in creating robust code but also ensures that your solution is ready for production scenarios.

Additionally, consider testing and validation as part of your prompt. Asking the model to generate test cases can further enhance the quality of the output. For example: "Write a Python function that calculates the factorial of a number, and include a few test cases to verify its correctness, including edge cases like 0 and negative numbers." By prompting the model to think about testing, you can derive outputs that are closer to what is needed in real-world applications.

By treating the model as a junior developer that requires thorough, stepwise instructions, you can extract technical outputs that are not only functional but also efficient, well-commented, and maintainable. A detailed and structured prompt leads to higher-quality code that meets specific needs, reducing the time required for subsequent modifications and debugging.

**NOTE**

*ChatGPT canvas mode is particularly useful for error handling. Its extended response capability allows you to provide a large code snippet and request detailed analysis of potential errors, debugging suggestions, and even explanations for why errors occur. It allows to highlight a certain part of the code and directly prompt for a solution regarding this exact junk of code. This helps streamline the troubleshooting process for complex codebases.*

# EIGHT

## Prompt Iteration and Testing

### *Iterative Refinement*

Creating an effective prompt is rarely a one-and-done task. Just like any other creative or technical process, getting the best possible output often requires iteration—the ongoing cycle of testing, tweaking, and refining your prompts to optimize the quality of the response. This iterative approach allows you to address ambiguities, adjust the level of detail, and enhance clarity, ultimately leading to outputs that are more aligned with your goals. In this section, we will delve into the art of iterative refinement, demonstrating how each cycle can bring you closer to your desired result.

### The Importance of Iteration

Iteration is at the heart of good prompt design. Think of each prompt as a draft—a starting point that evolves as you interact with the language model. Sometimes the first attempt might yield a response that's close to what you envisioned, but it's common to find that the output needs slight adjustments. By iteratively refining your prompt, you narrow the gap between your expectations and the model's output, making it increasingly precise and targeted.

For example, if you ask, "Explain how photosynthesis works," and the response is too broad or lacks specific details, you might refine the prompt to say, "Explain how photosynthesis works, focusing on the role of chlorophyll and the light-dependent reactions." This refinement helps guide the model more precisely toward the information you need.

The iterative process doesn't just involve adjusting the content; it can also mean modifying the tone, length, complexity, or even the structure of the response. Perhaps you wanted a friendly, conversational explanation, but the output sounded too formal. In that case, a simple adjustment like, "Explain photosynthesis in a friendly and engaging tone, suitable for middle school students", can make a huge difference. Each iteration is a step toward more effective communication with the language model, allowing you to tailor responses to specific needs.

**Techniques for Effective Refinement**

1. Analyze the Initial Output: The first step in refining a prompt is carefully analyzing the initial response. Identify elements that didn't quite meet your needs. Was there a lack of depth? Too much jargon? Inadequate structure? Pinpointing these issues allows you to make targeted changes that steer the model in the right direction.
2. Change One Variable at a Time: To understand the effect of a particular change, it's often best to adjust one aspect of your prompt at a time. If you simultaneously modify the tone, content focus, and response length, it's challenging to determine which change had the desired effect. Instead, tweak just one element—such as adding a specific instruction for tone—and then evaluate the impact. This controlled approach helps you understand exactly what works and what doesn't, leading to more predictable improvements.

3. Experiment with Different Approaches: Don't be afraid to experiment with completely different phrasing or techniques if your initial iterations aren't yielding satisfactory results. Sometimes a minor rewording can make a substantial difference. If "Describe the importance of biodiversity" results in an overly technical response, you might try, "Why is biodiversity important for maintaining healthy ecosystems? Answer in simple language." Experimentation is key to discovering the most effective phrasing and can often reveal new ways to improve clarity and relevance.

4. Consider the Audience: Always keep your audience in mind while iterating. A prompt that works well for a general audience might not be suitable for subject matter experts, and vice versa. When refining, think about whether your prompt matches the knowledge level, interests, and needs of your intended readers. For example, "Explain quantum computing" could be refined to "Explain quantum computing to someone with a basic understanding of physics but no knowledge of computer science." Tailoring the prompt to your audience ensures that the response is engaging and understandable, which is critical for effective communication.

## Practical Example of Iterative Refinement

Suppose you want to generate a list of healthy breakfast ideas for a blog post. You start with the prompt, "List some healthy breakfast ideas." The model might give you a list that includes familiar options like oatmeal, yogurt, and scrambled eggs. However, you were hoping for some more creative, less common suggestions. In this case, you could refine the prompt to say, "List ten unique and creative healthy breakfast ideas, focusing on plant-based ingredients and superfoods."

By iterating in this way, you can drive the output toward your specific expectations, encouraging creativity, novelty, and focus where you need it most. Iterative refinement allows you to continuously push the boundaries of what the language model can produce, resulting in increasingly engaging and customized outputs.

## Using Fragments for Refinement

One highly effective method for prompt refinement is using fragments from previous outputs to guide new iterations. By identifying what worked well—or didn't work—in a model's initial response, you can craft a revised prompt that incorporates these insights, ensuring the next version of the response improves upon the last.

### Fragment-Based Refinement: A Closer Look

Fragments are portions of a response that are either particularly effective or notably problematic. Let's say you receive a response to the prompt, "Explain how renewable energy works", and you particularly like the way the model explained solar energy but found the wind energy section lacking detail. In this case, you could create a new prompt like, "Explain how renewable energy works, using the same level of detail for wind energy as you did for solar energy in the previous response."

### Benefits of Using Fragments

- Highlighting Successes: Fragments help you pinpoint what was effective in an earlier response. If a particular analogy or example worked well, you can prompt the model to expand on that approach in other parts of the answer. This method not only leverages what's already working but also encourages the model to replicate successful elements across different parts of the response.

- Addressing Gaps: If the model's output was inconsistent, you can directly address these gaps by referring back to the successful parts. This makes the refinement process more efficient, as you're leveraging what already works while focusing specifically on the weaker sections that need improvement.

## Practical Application

Imagine you are writing educational content about the water cycle for young students. You start with the prompt, "Explain the water cycle in simple terms." The response effectively covers evaporation but gives a confusing explanation of condensation. You could refine the prompt by saying, "Explain the water cycle in simple terms, ensuring that the condensation stage is described as clearly as the evaporation stage in your previous answer." This way, you directly build on what was successful while addressing the weaker areas, ensuring that the entire explanation is cohesive and easy to understand.

## Iteration and Fragments: A Synergistic Approach

Combining iterative refinement with fragment-based techniques creates a powerful synergy for prompt optimization. Iteration allows you to progressively mold the response, while fragments provide concrete elements to focus on, either for replication or improvement. Together, these strategies help ensure that your prompts evolve effectively, leading to consistently high-quality outputs. By utilizing both methods, you are better equipped to refine prompts in a structured and efficient manner, ultimately enhancing the quality, clarity, and usefulness of the model's responses.

# NINE

## Combining Techniques for Optimal Results

### *Blending Techniques*

Combining different prompting techniques can lead to richer and more effective outcomes, especially when dealing with complex or nuanced tasks. Just as a chef combines multiple ingredients to create a dish that's more than the sum of its parts, you can blend prompting strategies to get optimal results from a large language model. By creatively mixing different approaches, you can effectively unlock the full potential of the model and tailor its responses to meet your specific needs. In this section, we will explore how blending various techniques—such as Chain-of-Thought (CoT), role assignments, step-by-step guidance, and example-driven prompting—can amplify the model's capabilities to meet a diverse array of objectives.

One approach to blending techniques is to use an example-driven prompt as a foundation while adding a step-by-step instruction layer. For instance, if your goal is to generate a detailed marketing strategy, you might start with a well-crafted example of a successful campaign and then guide the model step-by-step to build a similar campaign, tailored to a specific industry or demographic. The combination ensures that the model understands the structure while having the flexibility to adapt details according to context. This layered guidance prevents the model from getting lost in ambiguity and helps maintain focus throughout the task. Additionally, providing specific examples makes it easier for the model to generate content that is both relevant and actionable, while the step-by-step approach ensures a logical progression of ideas.

Another effective way to blend techniques is to pair role assignment with Chain-of-Thought (CoT) prompting. By assigning the model a specific role—such as an expert chef, an environmental scientist, or a project manager—you provide an overarching context that guides the nature of its responses. When you further incorporate CoT prompting, you encourage the model to articulate its reasoning within that specialized role, thereby producing richer, more comprehensive answers. For example, instructing the model to act as a project manager while solving a budgeting problem with CoT reasoning will lead to both practical and logically structured insights, because the assigned role shapes its assumptions and priorities. This kind of layered prompting can result in a response that not only solves the problem at hand but also provides additional context and rationale, making it more useful for decision-making.

Blending is also useful for managing tone and style. If you need an output that's both informative and emotionally engaging, you can combine direct instructional prompts with requests for empathetic, human-like language. For instance, while drafting a letter of encouragement, use a direct prompt for the message content and then add a refinement directive to make it more warm and compassionate. This approach helps to ensure that the response is both factually accurate and emotionally resonant, thereby enhancing its overall effectiveness. Similarly, combining a factual directive with a tone adjustment prompt can be particularly effective when writing for diverse audiences—ensuring that the content is both precise and appropriately nuanced for the reader.

When combining multiple techniques, iteration becomes key. You can start by testing an initial blended prompt, assessing its output, and then tweaking one or more of the layers to improve results. For instance, you might find that the example you provided is too narrow or that the step-by-step instructions need more elaboration. By iterating on your blended prompts, you can refine them to achieve the best possible outcome. The interplay between various methods can yield synergies that significantly enhance the model's performance—unlocking deeper creativity, better accuracy, and more targeted insights compared to using a single prompting technique. This iterative process is akin to refining a recipe: each adjustment can bring you closer to the desired result, ultimately yielding an outcome that is greater than the sum of its parts.

Blending techniques allows for flexibility, enabling the model to navigate tasks that are complex, multifaceted, or subjective. Just like how a craftsman selects the right tools for different parts of a project, you can select and combine various prompting methods to suit your specific needs. The art of blending prompts ultimately lies in understanding the strengths and weaknesses of each technique and finding the optimal combination that works harmoniously for the task at hand. Whether it's guiding the model through a logical analysis or encouraging it to generate creative ideas, blending techniques can be a powerful approach for achieving optimal results.

By thoughtfully combining different strategies, you can create prompts that are highly adaptive and effective. Whether tackling a creative writing challenge, a technical analysis, or a strategic planning task, using blended techniques enables the model to produce outputs that are more comprehensive, detailed, and tailored to your specific requirements. This flexibility not only allows you to handle a wide range of tasks but also ensures that the quality of the output remains consistently high. Blending techniques can transform a simple query into a multi-layered conversation, ultimately making the model a more capable and versatile tool in your workflow.

## Testing Multiple Models

When it comes to getting the best out of large language models (LLMs), one size definitely does not fit all. Testing multiple models is a key strategy for maximizing the quality of your outcomes, as each model comes with its own unique strengths and quirks. Imagine you're a chef, and each LLM is a different ingredient in your kitchen—some are spicy, others are sweet, and many have subtle undertones that you won't notice until you try them. By combining and testing different models, you can create a recipe that's perfectly balanced for your needs.

It's important to remember that LLMs have different training data, architectures, and inherent biases that make them perform better or worse depending on the context. For instance, you might find that one model excels at creative writing, generating beautiful metaphors and imaginative narratives, while another model shines when it comes to technical accuracy or providing well-sourced facts. By testing multiple models, you can determine which one is best suited for a specific task— whether it's crafting an evocative poem or conducting an in-depth technical analysis. Finding the right model can make all the difference.

A great way to start testing models is by selecting a core set of LLMs with distinct specialties. For example, you might choose a model like GPT-4 for its versatile creativity, another model that excels in conversational tone, and yet another that specializes in producing structured, technical content. Once you've selected your models, crafting the same prompt for each and observing the different outputs can be very enlightening. This approach helps you identify the model that's most effective for your purpose, while also providing valuable insight into how each model interprets language uniquely.

## LLM Cook-Off

Let's put a fun twist on this process. Imagine you're the host of a cooking competition, but instead of chefs, each contestant is an LLM. *Model A* steps up and serves a sizzling hot dish full of unexpected flavors—perhaps a dramatic story that has everyone on the edge of their seats. Next, *Model B* presents a carefully measured, step-by-step soufflé, with precision that would make a master baker proud. Finally, *Model C* walks in with a versatile sampler platter—there's a bit of storytelling, some well-seasoned facts, and a dash of humor that makes the judges smile. Testing multiple models is like being that host who gets to decide which dish deserves the blue ribbon for each type of meal you need.

## Surprises Along the Way

A useful tip when testing multiple models is to take note of the kinds of responses that surprise you, both positively and negatively. Some models may produce unexpected but brilliant insights, while others may completely misinterpret your prompt. The point is to remain open-minded. Often, the process is full of unexpected discoveries that can help refine your approach to prompting in general. Testing LLMs is also an excellent way to develop a better intuition about how subtle changes in prompts can lead to vastly different results.

When working on complex or multi-layered projects, the value of testing multiple models becomes even more evident. You may use one model for brainstorming, another for fact-checking, and a third for adding emotional depth or polishing the final text. Each model brings a specific talent to the table, and testing them helps you understand how to orchestrate these talents into one cohesive and effective output.

## Casting the Right Roles

Another entertaining way to think about testing multiple models is to imagine you're a movie director casting actors for different roles. Model A might be perfect for delivering a dramatic monologue, while Model B is the comedian who can add levity at just the right moment. Model C could be the narrator, tying everything together in a cohesive and engaging way. By testing each model, you're effectively casting the best performers for each part of your project, ensuring that the final production is as captivating and effective as possible.

## Staying Dynamic

Lastly, remember that new models are constantly being released, each boasting new capabilities and improvements. Testing multiple models is not a one-time effort; it's a dynamic process that adapts as technology advances. Just when you think you've figured out the perfect model for your needs, a new one might come along that's even better. So be prepared to occasionally return to the talent show, seeing if the latest contestants can outperform the ones you currently have in your lineup.

## Embrace the Experimentation

The key to effectively testing multiple models lies in curiosity and adaptability. You're not just a user—you're an experimenter, someone on the hunt for excellence in communication. Just like tasting different wines to find the perfect pairing, you need to take the time to explore and appreciate the nuances of each model. The process might take a little longer, but the payoff in terms of quality and creativity is more than worth it. Plus, there's a certain thrill in the discovery process, an excitement that comes from seeing how different models respond and bring your ideas to life in unexpected ways.

So, don't be afraid to mix things up, experiment, and see what each model can bring to the table. Whether you're creating art, solving complex problems, or simply looking for the best way to convey a message, testing multiple models can unlock new perspectives and possibilities. Embrace the adventure, and you just might find yourself delightfully surprised by what you discover.

## Fine-Tuning (prompt-based): Tailoring the Model to Your Needs

Fine-tuning is like taking a classic recipe and adjusting it to suit your own taste—adding a dash of this, a pinch of that—until it's perfect. When working with large language models, fine-tuning provides an opportunity to craft responses that align more closely with your specific needs, preferences, and the nuances of your projects. It's not just about making changes; it's about making the model truly yours, molding it until it feels like an extension of your own thinking and creativity.

Imagine you're tasked with training a chef who already knows the basics of cooking, but you need them to focus on a particular cuisine—let's say Italian. You would start with what the chef already knows, such as chopping, sautéing, and baking, and teach them specialized techniques, such as making pasta from scratch, perfecting sauces, or even learning to pick the freshest ingredients. In much the same way, fine-tuning an LLM involves taking a model that already has a foundation of knowledge and guiding it to specialize in the domain you need, whether that's conversational tone, technical detail, or creativity. This process allows you to leverage what the model already knows while adding layers of expertise that make it perfect for your specific use case.

Fine-tuning helps control not only the content but also the delivery. For instance, if your target audience prefers informal, easy-going explanations, fine-tuning allows you to imbue the model with a more laid-back, conversational style. On the other hand, if your audience is a group of legal experts, fine-tuning can help the model produce responses with appropriate complexity and accuracy, adhering to formal language standards. This targeted tailoring ensures the model's responses feel like they were written by someone in the right context, not a one-size-fits-all language bot. The ability to adapt style and tone makes the model much more effective at resonating with the intended audience.

Another important aspect of fine-tuning is handling context-specific language. Certain industries and fields have specialized jargon— technical words or phrases that mean one thing to insiders but might not be well-known to the public. In medicine, for example, the word "stat" means immediately. Fine-tuning allows an LLM to understand and accurately use these terms, making it sound like a native speaker within that specialized field. Whether it's legal language, medical jargon, or specific business terminology, a fine-tuned model is better equipped to understand and deliver accordingly. This ensures that the responses are not just technically correct but also contextually appropriate, giving the impression that the model is well-versed in the intricacies of the field.

Moreover, fine-tuning makes a significant difference when it comes to handling sensitivity and ethics. Consider an LLM intended for customer support in healthcare—it needs to understand how to respond empathetically, offering reassurances and comfort while still being factual and direct. Fine-tuning can guide the model to balance warmth with professionalism, avoiding responses that could come off as too mechanical or, conversely, too informal. This nuance is crucial for maintaining user trust and ensuring the model serves its purpose effectively. By fine-tuning the way a model handles sensitive topics, you can create a more human-centric experience, which is particularly important in fields like healthcare, where empathy is key.

An additional benefit of fine-tuning is improved efficiency. When a model is fine-tuned, it often becomes more efficient at providing relevant responses, simply because it has learned to focus on the areas that matter most for your use case. Imagine asking an unfocused, generic model about a legal matter; it might ramble through background information, missing the specific detail you needed. A fine-tuned model, by contrast, would jump straight to the point, offering targeted insights and omitting unnecessary filler. This streamlined approach not only saves time but also ensures that users get the information they need without the frustration of wading through irrelevant content.

Let's look at an example of fine-tuning in action. Suppose you are developing an AI assistant for a law firm specializing in intellectual property rights. Out of the box, an LLM may understand the basics of law but lack depth in the complexities of intellectual property nuances, such as patent disputes or trademark filings. By fine-tuning the model on relevant legal texts, case studies, and specialized terminology, you essentially educate it to become a quasi-expert in that field. The result? It can generate more insightful and accurate responses that meet the specific demands of a legal professional. This kind of precision makes the model an invaluable asset, as it can provide highly relevant information and assist with complex, domain-specific inquiries.

For instance, imagine the LLM being asked, "How can I protect my startup's brand name?" A generic model might provide a high-level overview of trademark registration, but a fine-tuned LLM that has been trained specifically on intellectual property law could give a more detailed answer, including the types of trademarks, how to perform a trademark search, and even common pitfalls that startups face in the registration process. This level of specificity transforms the model from a general assistant into a specialized advisor, offering targeted support that is far more useful for the end user.

Fine-tuning isn't just for text generation—it can also make technical tasks more manageable. For instance, if you use LLMs for coding assistance, fine-tuning can help the model adapt to your preferred coding standards, languages, and even personal conventions. Say you're a software team that uses a particular comment style or has certain preferences regarding variable naming. Fine-tuning can align the LLM with these specific requirements, turning it into a much more practical assistant that feels like an extension of your team, rather than a tool you need to adapt to constantly. This personalization makes the model far more useful and intuitive, allowing it to integrate seamlessly into your workflow.

For example, imagine you're a Python developer who prefers using snake_case for variable names and has strict guidelines for code documentation. A generic LLM might generate code that doesn't adhere to these conventions, requiring additional editing. However, a fine-tuned model trained on your team's codebase would automatically generate code that fits your style, complete with well-formatted docstrings and consistent variable names. This kind of alignment saves time and reduces friction, making the model a more efficient collaborator.

Fine-tuning takes patience—it involves retraining parts of the model with new data and testing to ensure the desired effects are achieved. But much like how an artist meticulously refines each detail of a sculpture until it matches their vision, fine-tuning results in a model that fits your needs with almost customized precision. The payoff is a model that's both capable and context-aware, significantly enhancing the quality of your LLM applications. Whether you need the model to adhere to specific technical standards, communicate with empathy, or master industry-specific jargon, fine-tuning is the key to unlocking its full potential and ensuring that it works exactly the way you need it to.

# TEN

## Beyond the Obvious: Little-Known LLM Capabilities That Make Your Life Easier

Artificial Intelligence is revolutionizing the way we interact with technology, yet its potential remains vastly underexplored by most people. Modern large language models (LLMs), such as ChatGPT-4, PaLM 2, and Claude, offer remarkable capabilities that extend far beyond drafting emails or answering queries. In this chapter, we learn about some unexpected yet highly practical tasks these AI systems can perform, tasks that could redefine how we approach everyday tasks.

**Designing for the Future: Generating STL Files for 3D Printing**

Imagine describing a simple object—a simple keychain with your initials or a minimalist pen holder—and having a 3D model ready for printing. With AI, this is totally possible. By providing a detailed prompt, you can generate STL files for 3D printers (so called .gcode-Files), enabling you to bring ideas to life without any CAD knowledge.

Practical Example:
"Design me a compact phone stand that can hold both a phone and a stylus. Provide a '.gcode' file for download."

LLMs like ChatGPT-4, (sometimes paired with design tools such as Blender or Fusion 360), excel in creating detailed descriptions that can then be converted into printable models. Claude by Anthropic also shines in crafting the conceptual foundations of such designs.

**Streamlined Workflows: Automating Document Creation**

Drafting reports, resumes, or personalized letters can be tedious, but AI simplifies the process by automating document creation. Whether it's a business report with specific formatting or a thank-you letter, LLMs can produce professional-grade Word files in moments.

Practical Example:
"Create a project report template with sections for objectives, methodology, results, and recommendations. Provide a well formatted Word file for download"

ChatGPT-4 allows you to create downloadable DOCX files. For streamlined content organization, Claude is another excellent choice but might need a file-handler, depending on the version.

**Image Description and Analysis**

Modern LLMs can analyze and interpret images, providing detailed descriptions, artistic insights, or suggested captions. This capability is invaluable for accessibility, stock photography, or even marketing purposes.

Practical Example:
"Describe the scene in this photograph and suggest a poetic caption for social media." or "Describe the concept presented in the image at hand."

GPT-4 Vision, with its multi-modal capabilities, excels at identifying objects and explaining their context. DALL-E 3 complements this by offering artistic interpretations, making it ideal for creative applications.

**Solving Complex Problems: Interactive Code Debugging**

For programmers, debugging is often a frustrating process. AI transforms this challenge into a collaborative experience, diagnosing errors, suggesting fixes, and even improving overall code efficiency.

Practical Example:
"Here's a Python script with a KeyError issue. Fix it and add error handling to prevent future crashes."

ChatGPT-4's Code Interpreter is exceptional for such tasks, offering clear guidance and actionable fixes. GitHub Copilot, when integrated into development environments, provides hands-on support directly within your workflow.


**Writing Web Scraping Scripts**

Need specific information from a website? AI can generate Python scripts tailored to extract data while adhering to ethical guidelines.

Practical Example:
"Write a script to scrape job titles and company names from **a job portal**, and save them as a CSV file."

ChatGPT-4 and LLaMA 2 are both effective for generating scripts using libraries like BeautifulSoup or Scrapy, ensuring efficient and targeted data extraction.

**Fine-Tuning Interactions: Prompt Analysis and Optimization**

The key to effective AI interaction often lies in crafting the perfect prompt. AI can analyze and refine prompts, making them clearer, more structured, and optimized for better outcomes.

Practical Example:
"How can I improve this prompt: 'Explain the basics of quantum mechanics to a 10-year-old'?"

Both ChatGPT-4 and Claude are powerful assistants in optimizing prompts, offering insightful suggestions to improve clarity and specificity.


**Presentations: Automated Slide Creation**

Creating presentations can be time-consuming, but AI simplifies the process by drafting structured outlines with slide titles, bullet points, and even suggested visuals.

Practical Example:
"Draft a Powerpoint presentation outline for 'The Future of Renewable Energy' with 10 slides, each focusing on a key topic."

ChatGPT-4 provides detailed content for each slide, while Claude's logical structuring ensures your presentation has a natural flow.

# BONUS

## Modern State-of-the-Art Large Language Models (LLMs): A referenced List

**GPT-4o by OpenAI:** A multimodal model capable of processing and generating text, images, and audio, offering advanced reasoning and multilingual support. [1].

**Llama 3 by Meta AI:** An open-source model trained on a vast dataset, designed for versatility in various applications. [2].

**Nova by Amazon:** A series of AI foundation models integrated into AWS, including Nova Canvas for image generation and Nova Reel for video generation. [3].

**Claude 3 by Anthropic:** Focuses on safety and reliability, offering enhanced performance in understanding and generating human-like text. [4].

**Gemini 1.5 Pro by Google DeepMind:** Provides improved performance across various tasks and modalities, including text and image processing. [5].

**Mistral 7B by Mistral AI:** A compact yet powerful model excelling in language understanding and generation tasks. [6].

**DBRX by Databricks:** An open-source LLM designed for high performance in language understanding, programming, and mathematics. [7].

106

**Orion-14B by OrionStar AI:** A multilingual model trained on a diverse corpus, achieving state-of-the-art performance across various tasks. [8].

**MaLA-500 by Glot500:** Designed to cover an extensive range of 534 languages, bridging the gap for low-resource languages. [9].

**Phi-2 by Cohere:** Offers advanced language generation capabilities with a focus on coherence and relevance. [10].

**References:**

[1]: https://openai.com/index/hello-gpt-4o/

[2]: https://ai.meta.com/blog/meta-llama-3/

[3]: https://www.theverge.com/2024/12/3/24312260/amazon-nova-foundation-ai-models-anthropic

[4]: https://www.anthropic.com/claude

[5]: https://www.unite.ai/best-large-language-models-llms/

[6]: https://www.multimodal.dev/post/best-large-language-models-of-2024

[7]: https://www.databricks.com/blog/introducing-dbrx-new-state-art-open-llm

[8]: https://arxiv.org/abs/2401.12246

[9]: https://arxiv.org/abs/2401.13303

[10]: https://www.cohere.com/phi-2

Now that you've reached the end of this guide, you're equipped with a toolkit of strategies to unlock the potential of AI through skilled prompt engineering. From essential foundations to advanced techniques, you've explored how to craft prompts that yield clear, effective results.

Prompt engineering is both an art and an evolving skill—one that grows as AI technology progresses. Continue experimenting, refining, and adapting your prompts to meet new challenges and seize emerging opportunities.

Thank you for embarking on this journey. May your prompts inspire, your insights deepen, and your results continue to impress. Here's to shaping the future of AI, one prompt at a time.

*"CRAFTING PROMPTS IS LIKE TEACHING YOUR AI A DANCE—IT'S ALL ABOUT THE RIGHT MOVES, WITHOUT STEPPING ON EACH OTHER'S TOES!"*

**4o**

Printed in Great Britain
by Amazon